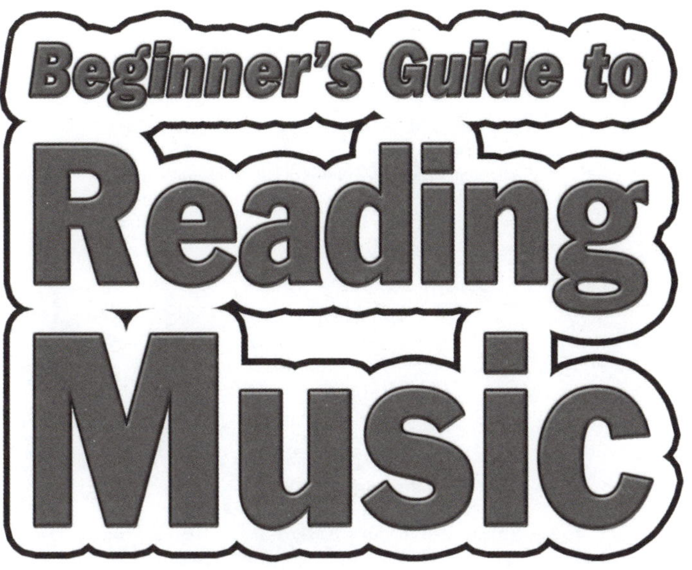

Beginner's Guide to Reading Music

Easy-to-Use • Easy-to-Learn

Simple Introduction For All Ages

Jake Jackson

FLAME TREE
PUBLISHING

Publisher and Creative Director: Nick Wells
Senior Editor: Catherine Taylor
Layout Design & Notation: Jake Jackson

Special thanks to Alan Brown for the scales notation
and Alex Davidson

21
9 10 8

This edition first published 2011 by
FLAME TREE PUBLISHING
6 Melbray Mews
Fulham, London SW6 3NS
United Kingdom
www.flametreepublishing.com

Music website: www.flametreemusic.com

ISBN 978-1-84786-950-0

A CIP record for this book is available from the British Library
upon request.

Acknowledgements
All chord diagrams and notation © Jake Jackson 2012, 2021.
Decorations and section openers courtesy of Flame Tree Studio.

Jake Jackson is a musician and writer of practical music books. His publications include *Advanced Guitar Chords*; *Chords for Kids*; *Classic Riffs*; *Guitar Chords*; *How to Play Electric Guitar*; *Piano and Keyboard Chords*; *Scales and Modes* and *The Songwriter's Rhyming Dictionary*.

Printed in China

Introducing the 12 steps

Organized into **12 easy steps,** this new book begins with the **basic concepts** and finishes with a compendium of symbols.

The first section introduces you to the **stave**, **notes** and **rests** before moving on to **key signatures** and **time signatures**. The large sections on **scales** and **chords** will expand your knowledge and help you to explore further.

This **beginner's guide** can also be used as a reminder of **basic musical terms**.

Contents

1
2
3
4
5
6
7
8
9
10
11
12

1
The Basics
Step One

Music is created by people singing and playing a wide variety of instruments. Writing down and reading the music is an important part of **music-making**.

The following pages will introduce you to the very basic concepts: what is a **stave**? what are **lines** and **spaces**? what are **ledger lines** and **clefs**?

This section closes with the note called **middle C**, the understanding of which will give you a solid foundation for the rest of the book.

1

9

1 2 3 4 5 6 7 8 9 10 11 12

Stave or Staff

These five lines make up the stave (sometimes called staff).

The stave is the backbone to the body of the music, it holds the **notes** and the **rests** and the various **symbols** that tell you how to play loudly or softly, when to repeat and when to stop.

The stave allows us to indicate **pitch**, whether a sound is high or low.

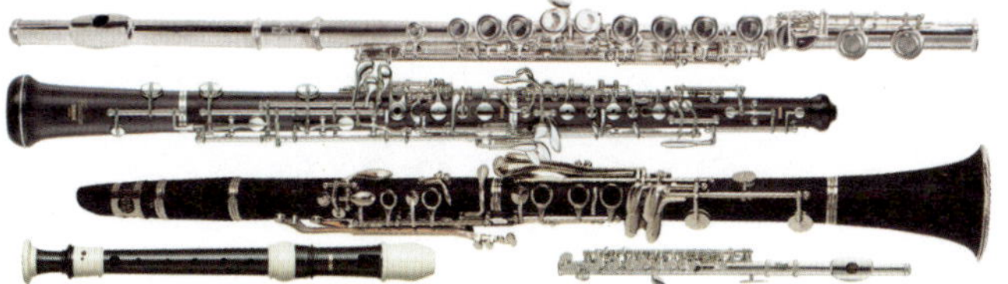

The **highest** sounds appear at the top of a stave.

The **lowest** sounds appear at the bottom of a stave.

Lines

The stave is always made up of **five** lines. Notes can be written on the lines or the spaces.

Each line on a stave represents a particular musical note, although which note depends on which **clef** is shown at the beginning of the music (clefs are covered on pages 20-25).

It is worth noting that the lines also show the music **moving** in time from **start** to **finish**, and should always be read from **left** to **right**.

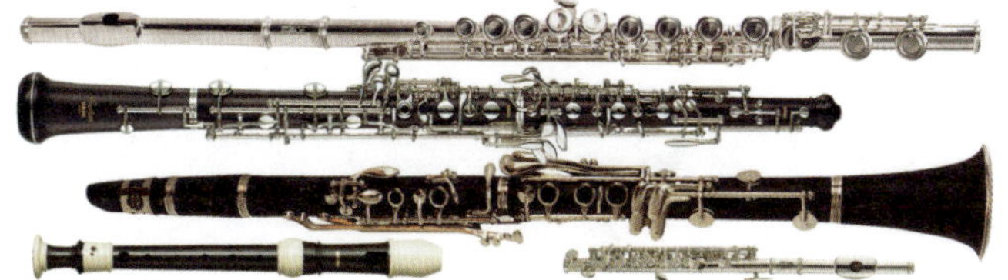

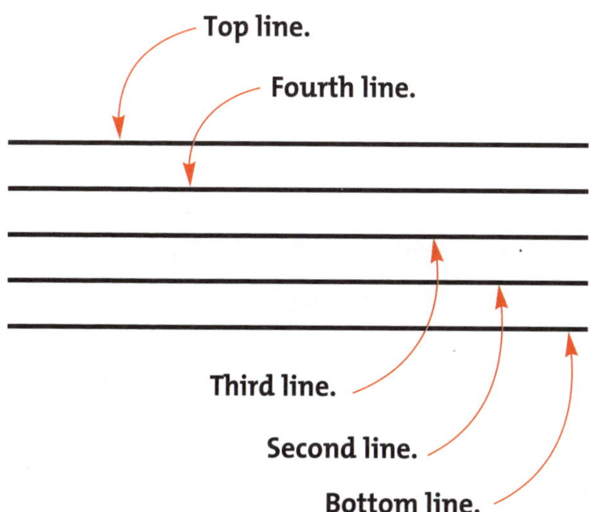

1 2 3 4 5 6 7 8 9 10 11 12

Spaces

Between the five lines there are four spaces. Notes can be placed in these spaces. The **higher** the **space** in the stave, the **higher** the **note**.

Notes can be placed on **both** the lines and the spaces.

There are spaces **above** and **below** the stave. These can also hold notes.

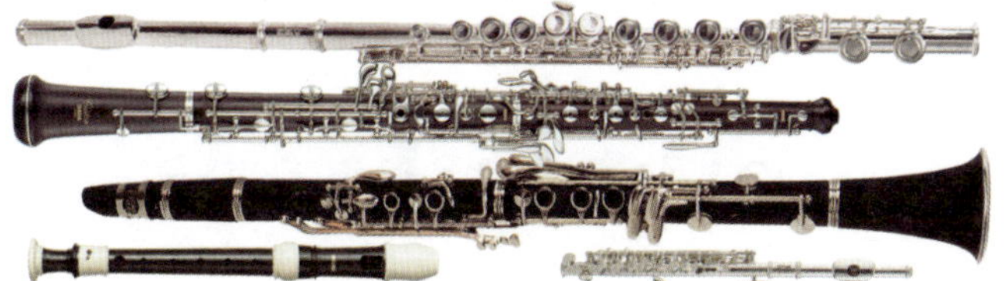

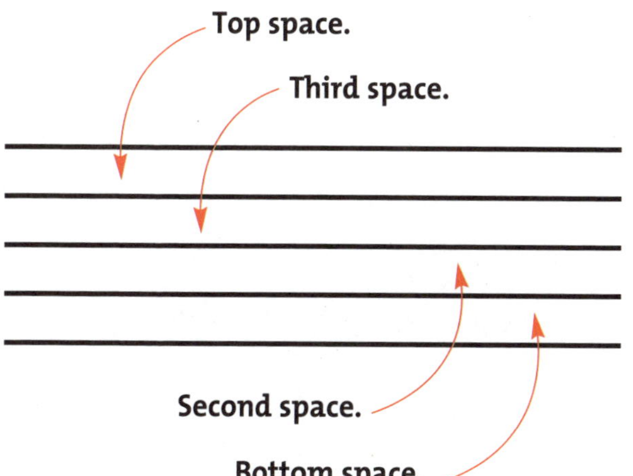

1 2 3 4 5 6 7 8 9 10 11 12

1 2 3 4 5 6 7 8 9 10 11 12

Ledger Lines

Often you will see music with small lines written above or below the main part of the stave. These are called **ledger lines**.

Ledger lines are only used when a note is written in a **space** or on a **line** where the note is higher or lower than those on the main part of the stave.

Ledger lines are written at equal distances from the main lines.

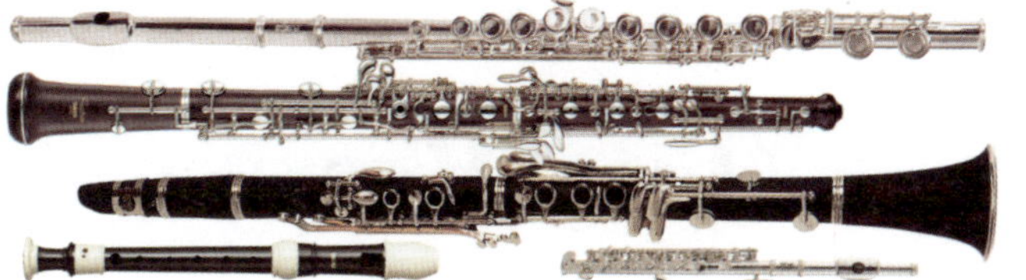

Notes higher than the stave can appear here.

Notes lower than the stave can appear here.

The Bars

When you look at music you will normally see a series of **vertical lines** placed at intervals along the stave. These are called **bar lines**.

The area between each barline is called a **bar**. Sometimes these are called **measures**.

Written music, called **notation**, is grouped into bars to provide structure to the notes, to make it easier to follow, and to show the **beat** of the music.

The **first bar** on each stave on a page of music always carries a **clef** symbol in place of the first bar line.

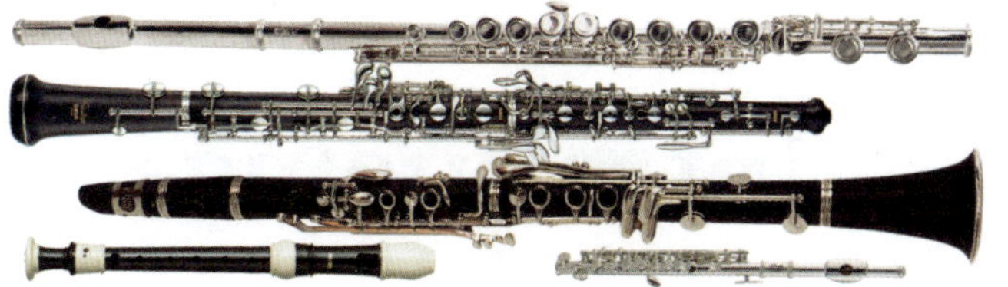

These are bars.

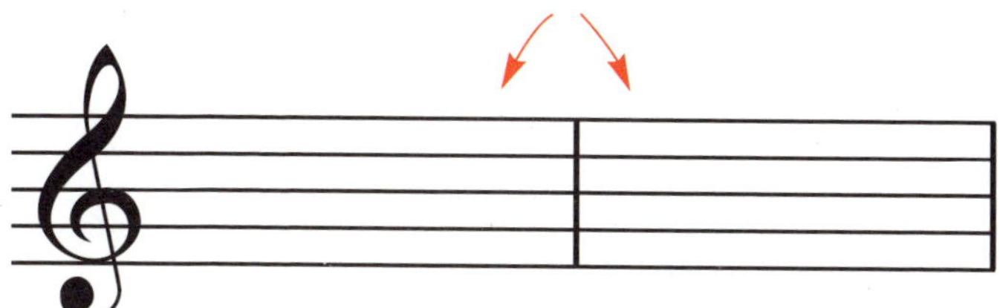

These are bar lines.

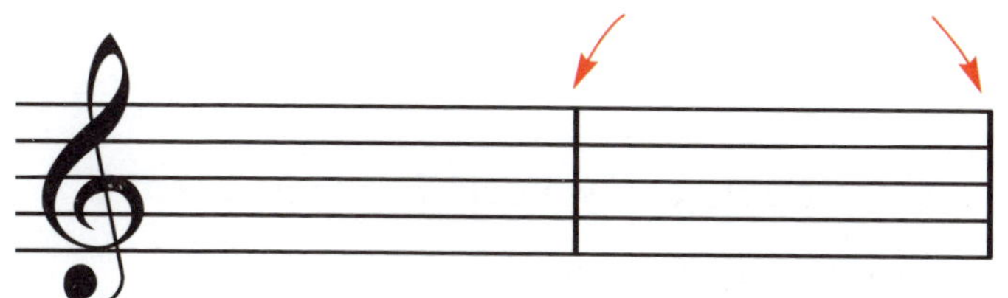

This is a treble clef.

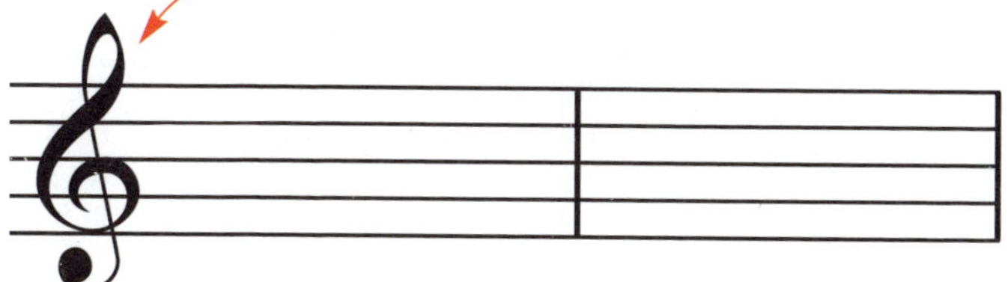

1 2 3 4 5 6 7 8 9 10 11 12

Introducing the Treble Clef

A clef symbol is written at the beginning of a piece of music, and at the beginning, on the left side, of every stave.

The **treble clef** is used for instruments that sound higher, usually above **middle C**.

The treble clef always **curls** around the **second line** from the bottom of the stave.

Instruments that commonly use the treble clef are the violin, guitar, treble recorder, saxophone, trumpet and the right hand on a piano.

Children's and female **voices** use the treble clef.

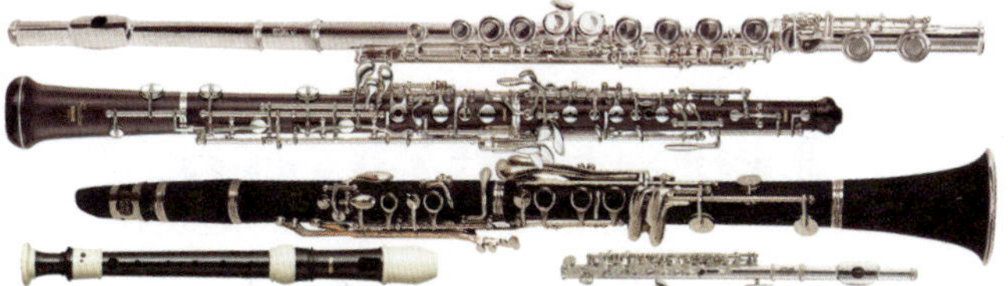

The curl of the treble clef wraps around the second line up from the bottom line.

Numbered from the bottom line upwards.

1 2 3 4 5 6 7 8 9 10 11 12

Introducing the Bass Clef

The bass clef is used for instruments and voices which sound **lower**, especially those that provide the bass sounds in a piece of music.

The bass clef is always written so that the two dots sit either side of the fourth line up from the bottom of the stave.

Instruments that commonly use the bass clef are the cello, bassoon, tuba, bass guitar and the left hand on a piano or any other keyboard instrument, such as an organ.

Male baritone, tenor and bass **voices** use the bass clef.

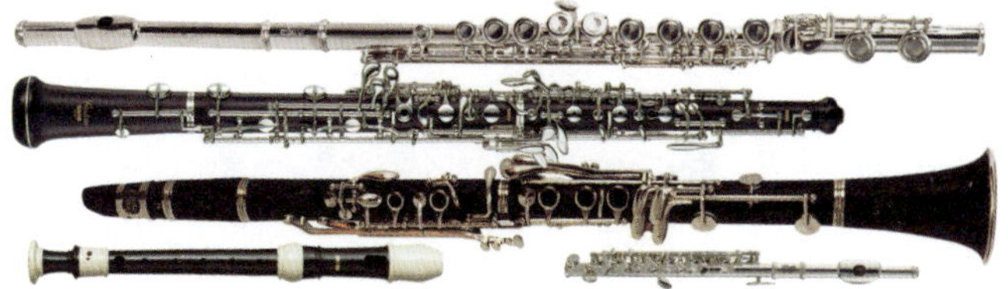

The two dots of the bass clef sit either side of fourth line up from the bottom line.

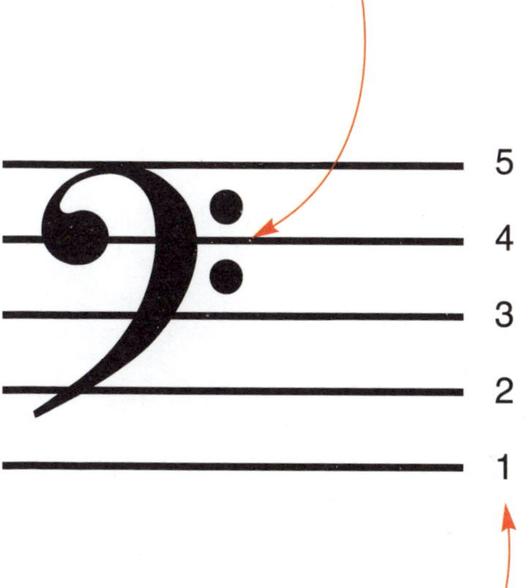

Numbered from the bottom line upwards.

The C Clef

Other clefs are occasionally used for different instruments to make the reading of them easier. These include the **alto clef** and the **tenor clef** (also called C clefs).

The **alto clef** can be used by the viola. The middle of this clef sits on the line that normally holds the middle C.

The **tenor clef** can used by the cello, bassoon and trombone. It also sits on the line of the middle C but the five bar lines shift down to provide a space and line below the botom edge of the clef.

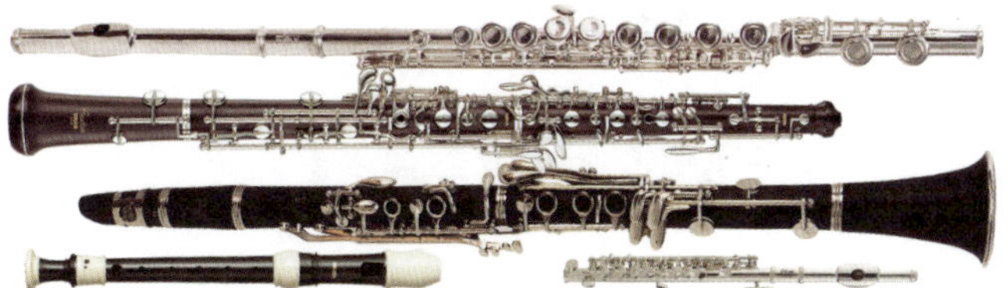

The middle of the **alto clef** sits on the line that normally shows middle C.

Numbered from the bottom line upwards.

Middle C

The note called middle C appears in the **middle** of the **piano**. It is usually the **lowest note** that an instrument using a **treble clef** can play.

Middle C appears on the first ledger line **below** the **treble clef** and the first ledger line **above** the **bass clef**. Middle C sits exactly between the treble and bass clef staves.

To make the reading and writing of notation easier, the gap between the staves of the treble and bass clef is usually stretched out to allow a middle C on **both** staves.

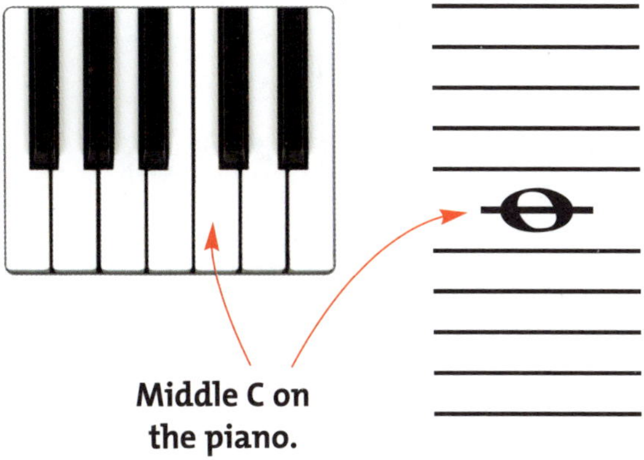

Middle C on the piano.

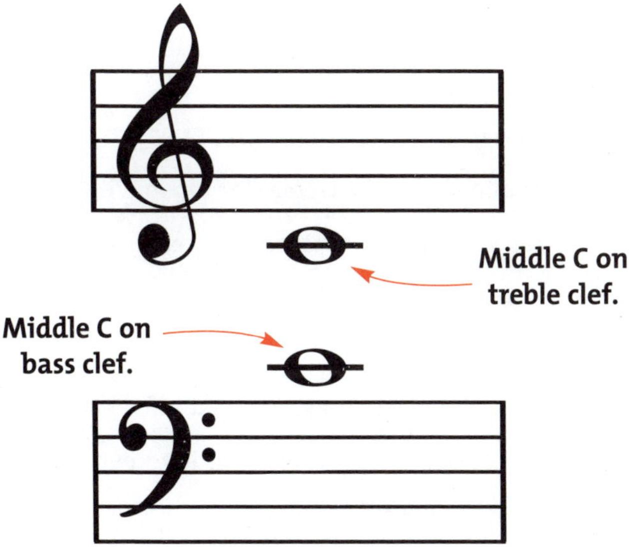

Middle C on treble clef.

Middle C on bass clef.

2

Treble Clef

Step Two

The treble clef is used for notes above **middle C**. On the **piano** this applies generally to the music played with the **right hand**.

Instruments such as the trumpet, violin and the clarinet also use the treble clef, along with higher voices such as the soprano (or treble) sounds of children and female singers.

This chapter offers more detailed information on the treble clef and provides ways to remember the notes of the lines and spaces.

Treble Clef Line Notes

A good way to remember the names for those notes that appear on the lines of the **treble clef** is to use a mnemonic to remind you:

Food

Deserves

Boy

Good

Every

Read from the bottom up.

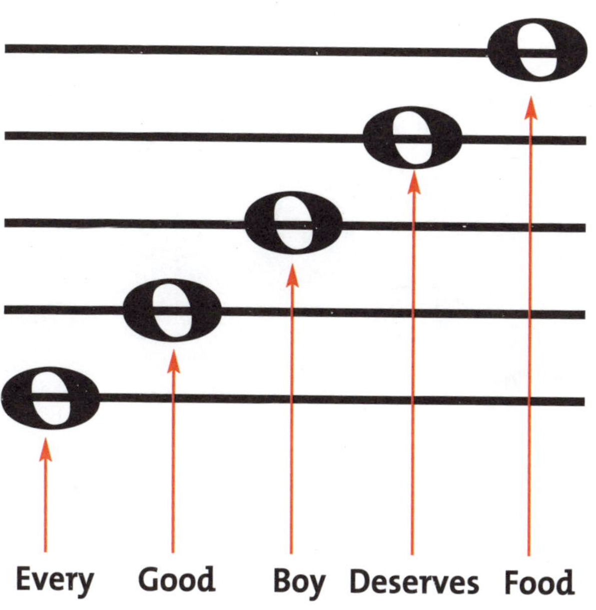
Every
Good
Boy
Deserves
Food

Treble Clef Line Notes on Keyboard

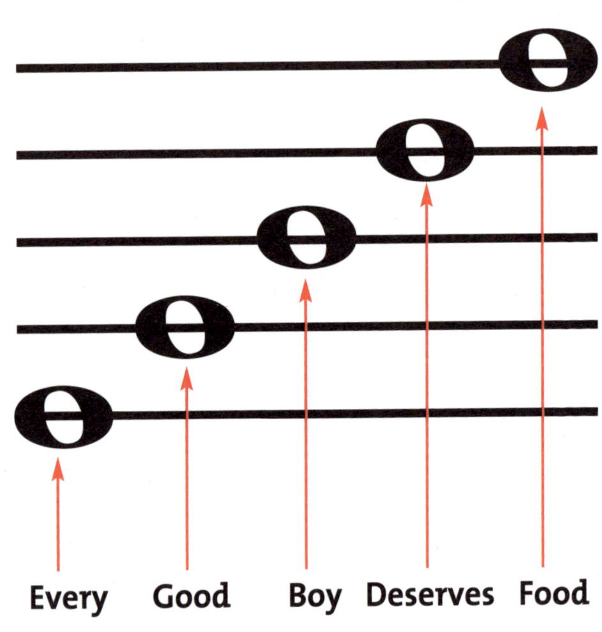

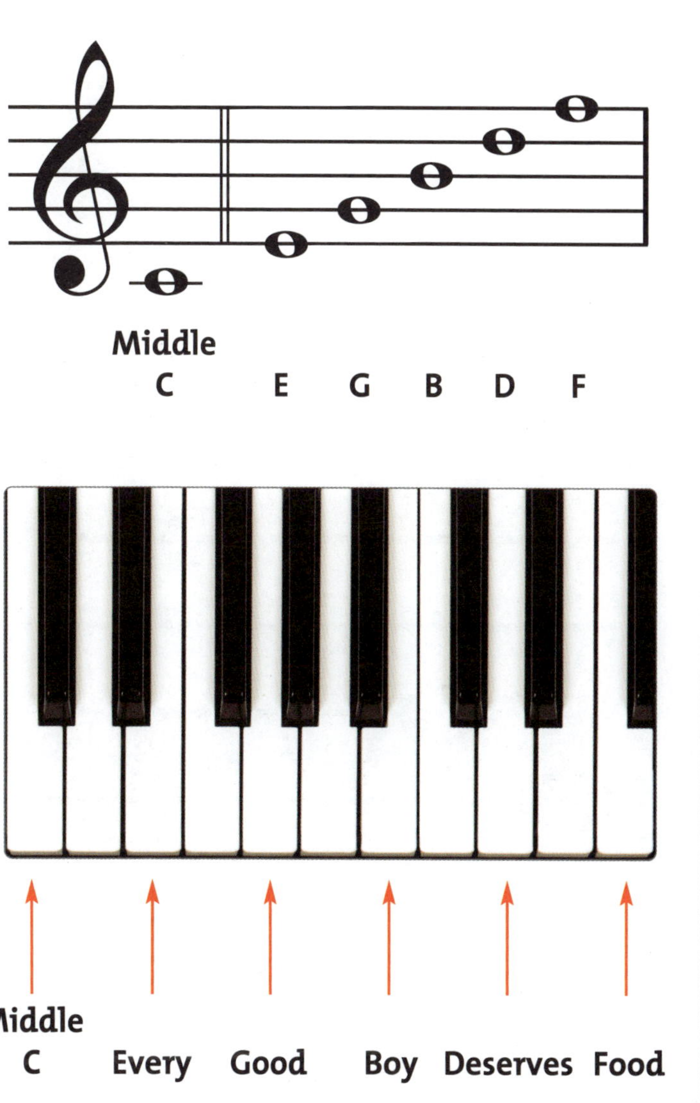

1
2
3
4
5
6
7
8
9
10
11
12

Treble Clef Line Notes on Guitar

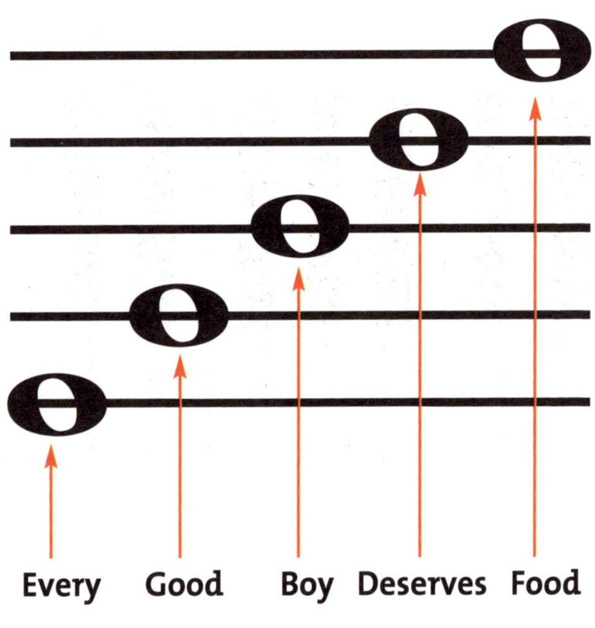

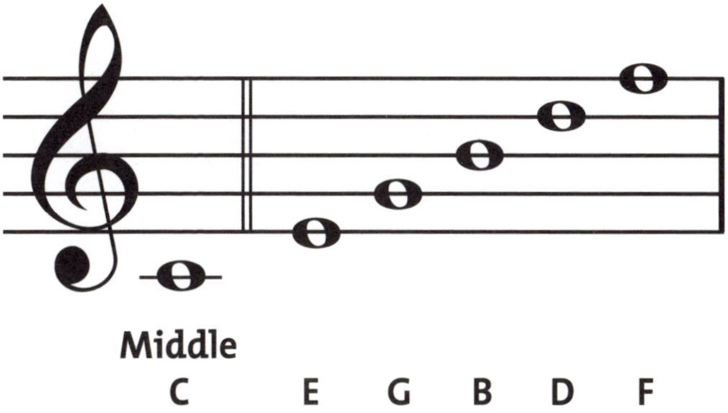

Middle
C E G B D F

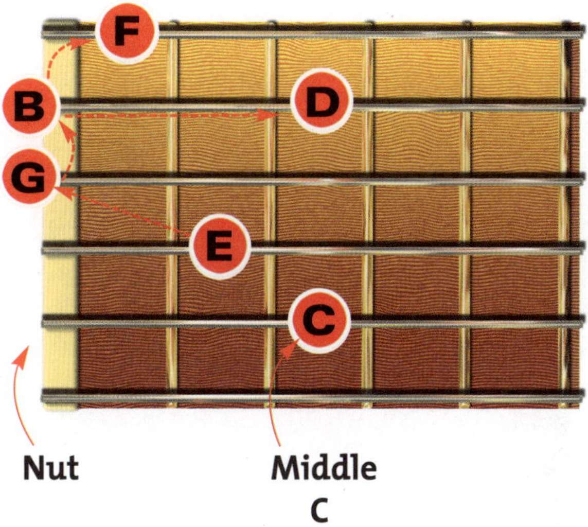

F
B D
G
E
C

Nut

Middle
C

The diagram here is from the player's view. Treble clef line notes on a guitar are spread across the strings. The notes G and B are shown here on the open strings.

Treble Clef Space Notes

You can use a similar method to remember those notes that appear in the spaces of the **treble clef**. They spell out a simple word:

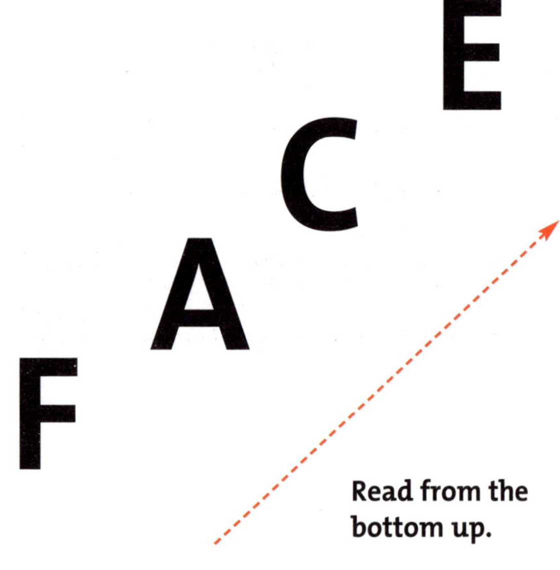

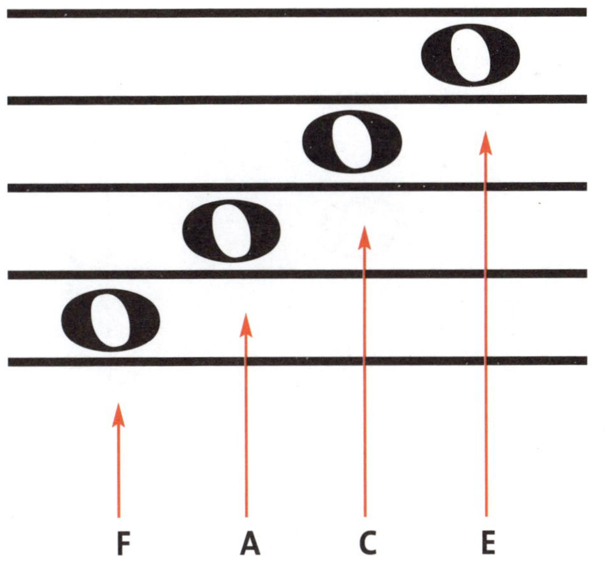
F
A
C
E

Treble Clef Space Notes on Keyboard

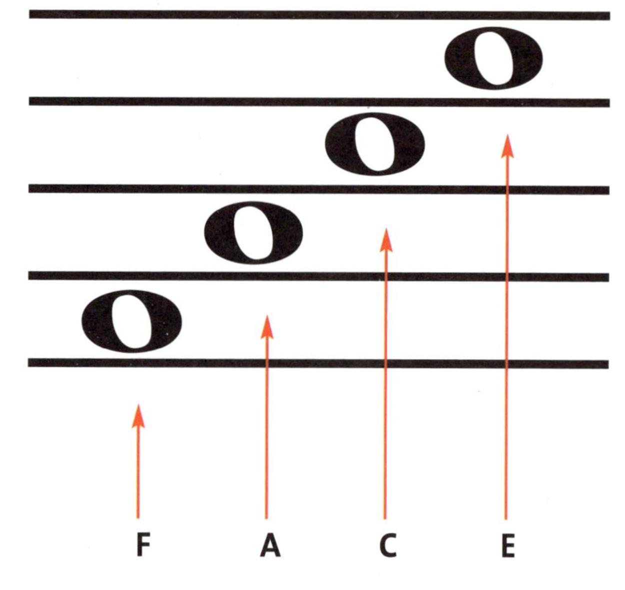

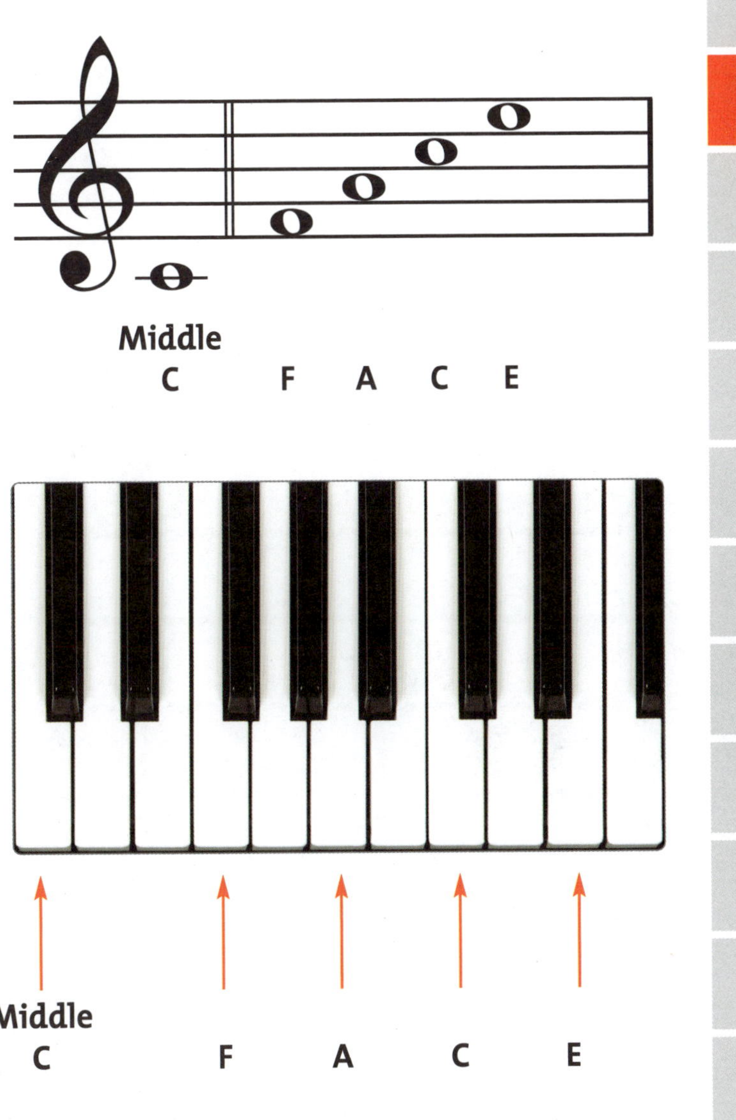

1 2 3 4 5 6 7 8 9 10 11 12

Treble Clef Space Notes on Guitar

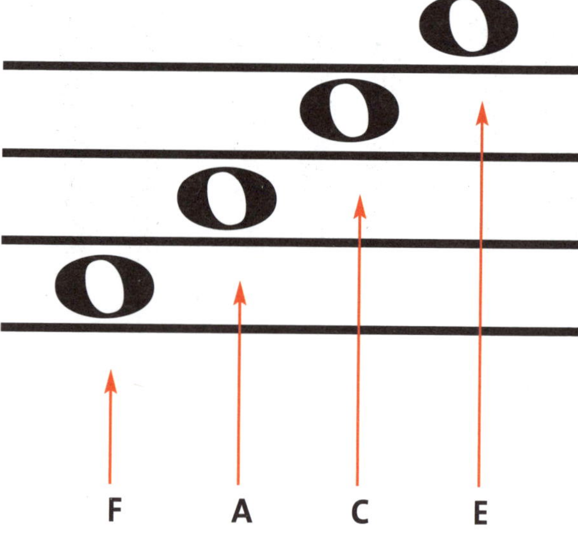

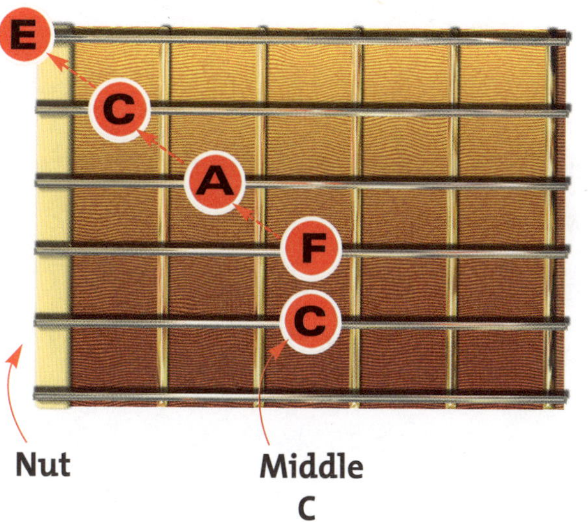

Again, the diagram here is from the player's view with the treble clef open notes played across the strings. The top note E is shown here on the open string.

Octaves

From the previous pages you might have noticed that the note names appear more than once on a stave. For instance, in the treble clef, in the spaces between the lines, the **C** of **F A C E** is **above middle C**, which sits **below** the stave.

This occurs because, in standard western music, there are **7** whole **note names**, from **A** to **G**, which are then repeated.

If you listen to the sound of middle C and the sound of the C above, you will hear that they have the same quality. The **interval** between notes of the same name is called an **octave**. When notes of the same name are played together they create a rich, enhanced sound.

The interval between the two C notes is an **octave**.

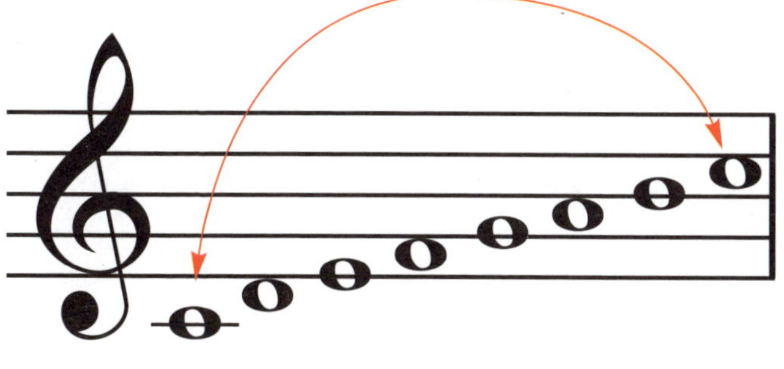

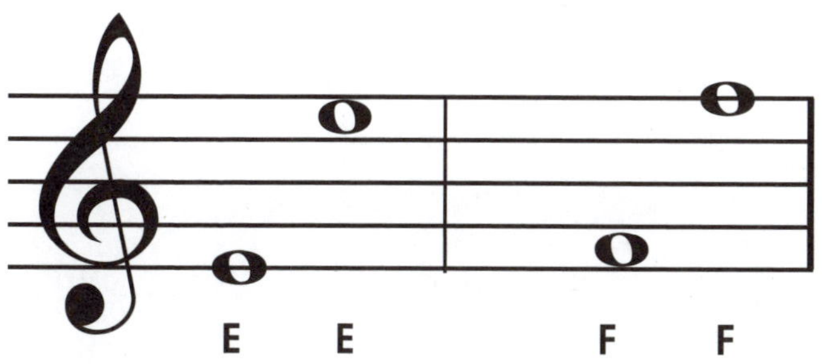

Examples of other **octaves**.

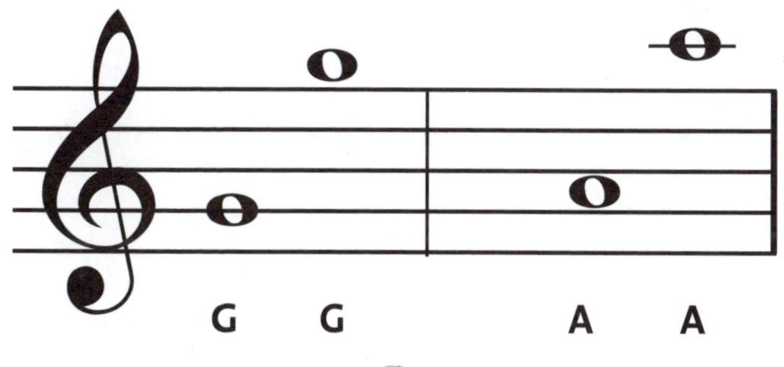

1 2 3 4 5 6 7 8 9 10 11 12

Notes Below the Treble Clef Stave

It is very useful to know how to work out the names of the notes **below** middle C.

Remember that the notes start at the bottom, so the **higher** the **position** of the note on the stave, the **higher** the **note**.

Remember also that these notes usually **only** appear on the ledger lines **if** there is **no bass clef**.

However, in piano music, **ledger lines** are sometimes used to signify that the notes should be played by the **right hand**, with the **bass clef** being reserved for the **left hand**.

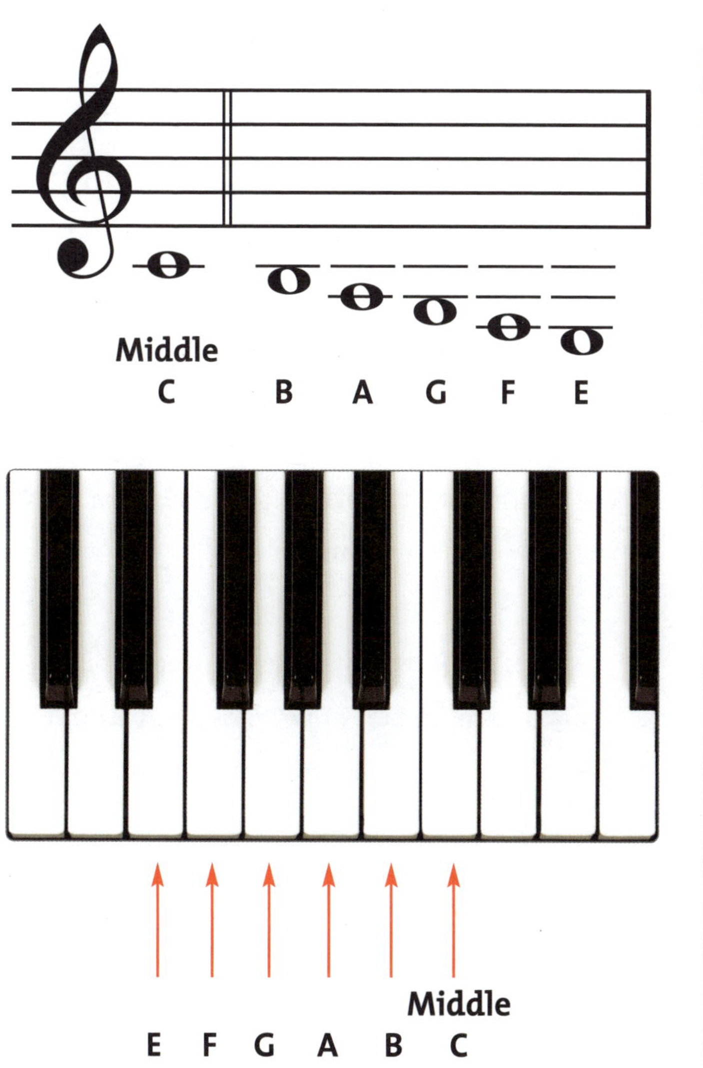

1
2
3
4
5
6
7
8
9
10
11
12

1
2
3
4
5
6
7
8
9
10
11
12

Notes Above the Treble Clef Stave

It is also useful to know how to work out the names of the notes above the stave.

Remember that the notes start at the bottom, so the **higher** the **position** of the note on the stave, the **higher** the **note**.

The notes **above** the stave can be worked out in relation to middle C. For instance the **A above** the stave can be called the **second A above** middle C.

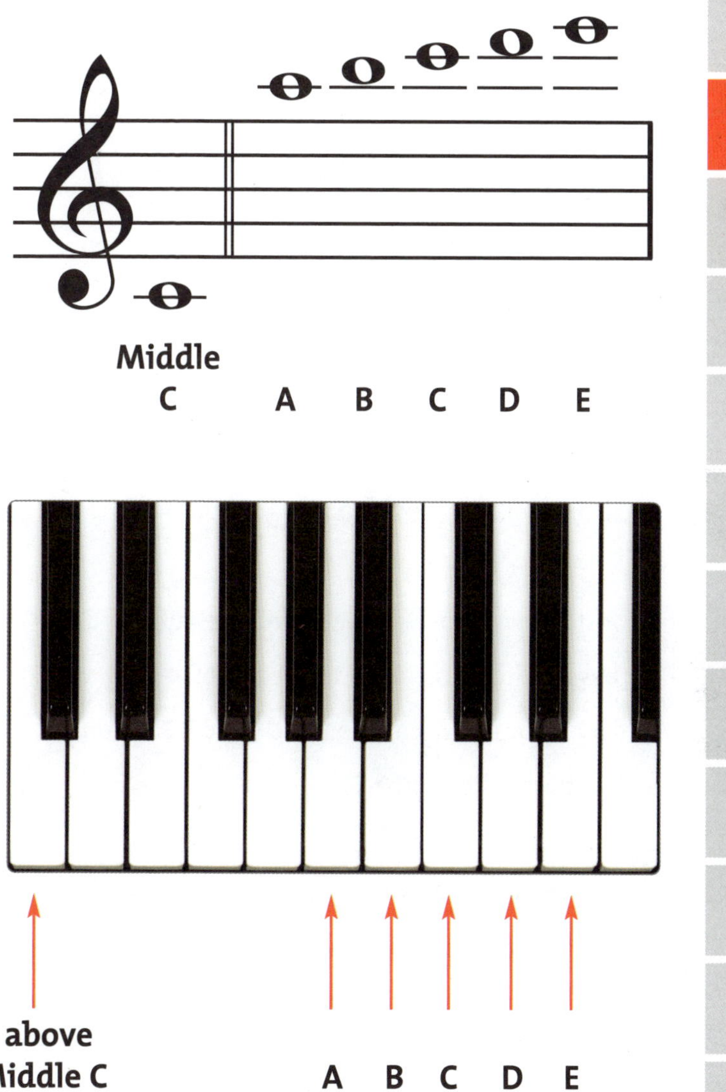
Middle
C
A
B
C
D
E
C above
Middle C
A
B
C
D
E

1
2
3
4
5
6
7
8
9
10
11
12

3

The Bass Clef

Step Three

The bass clef is used for notes below **middle C**. On the **piano** this applies generally to the music played with the **left hand**.

Instruments such as the trombone, tuba and the bass guitar also use the bass clef, along with lower voices such as the **tenor** and **bass** sounds of adult male **singers**.

This chapter offers more detailed information on the bass clef and provides ways to remember the notes on the lines and spaces.

Bass Clef Line Notes

As with the treble clef, a good way to remember the names for those notes that appear on the lines of the **bass clef** is to use a mnemonic to remind you:

Anything

Forget

Don't

Boys

Good

Read from the bottom up.

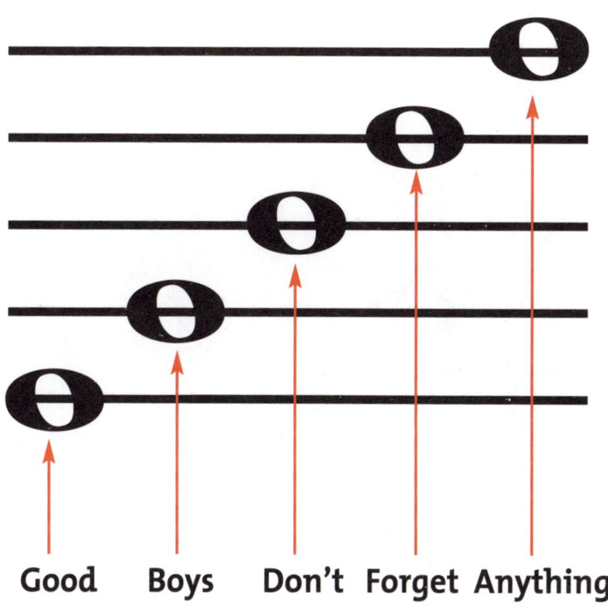
Good
Boys
Don't
Forget
Anything

1
2
3
4
5
6
7
8
9
10
11
12

Bass Clef Line Notes on Keyboard

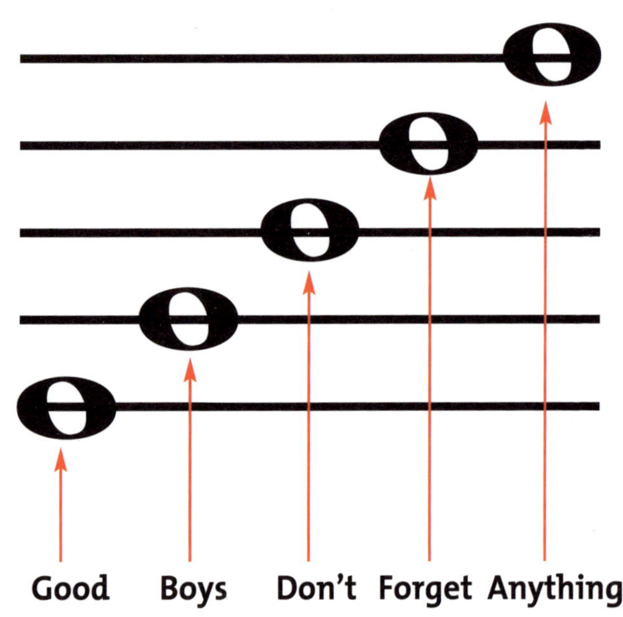

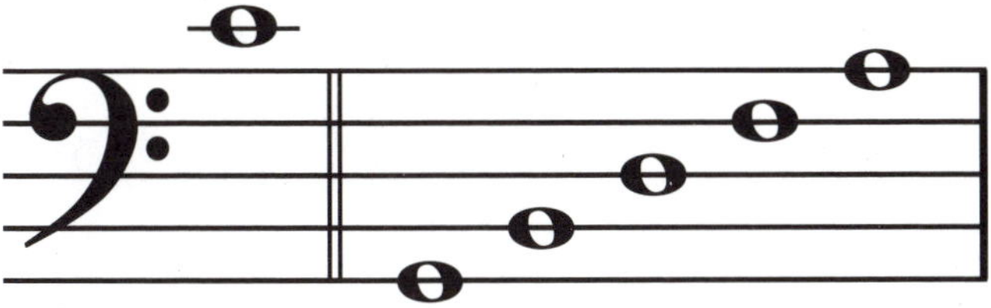

Middle
C G B D F A

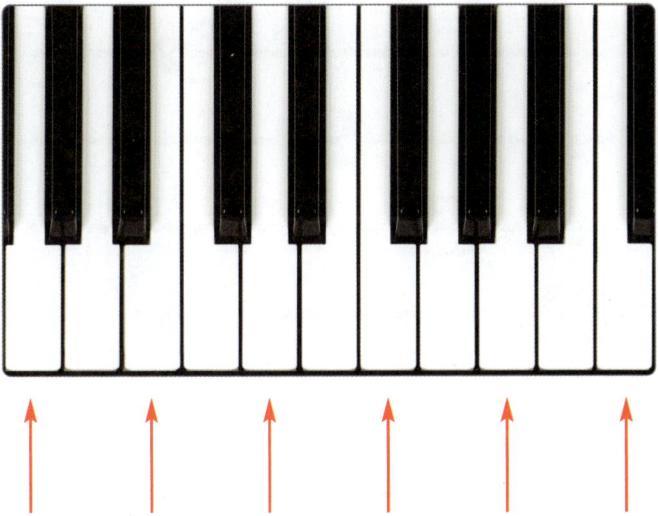

Good Boys Don't Forget Anything Middle C

Bass Clef Line Notes on Guitar

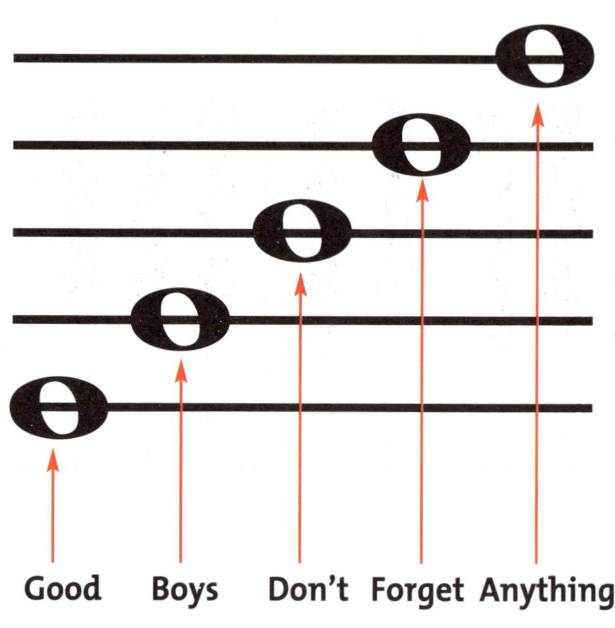

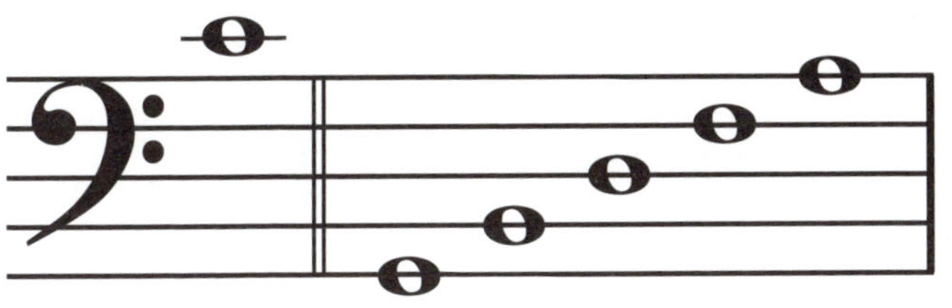

Middle
C G B D F A

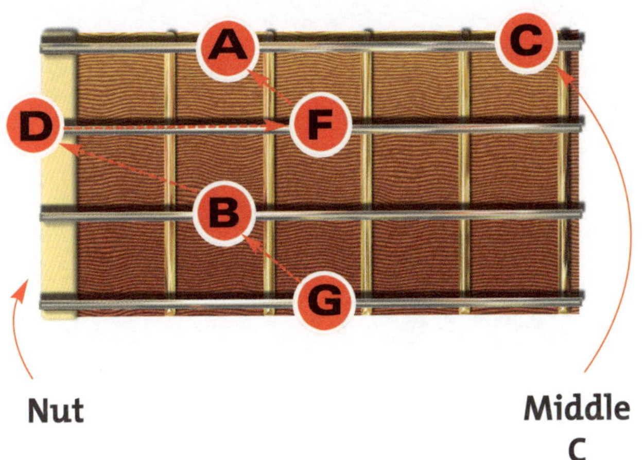

The diagram here is from the player's view. Bass clef line notes on a bass guitar are spread across the strings. The note D is shown on the open string.

1 2 3 4 5 6 7 8 9 10 11 12

Bass Clef Space Notes

As with the treble clef, a good way to remember the names for those notes that appear on the lines of the **bass clef** is to use a mnemonic to remind you:

Grass

Eat

Cows

All

Read from the bottom up.

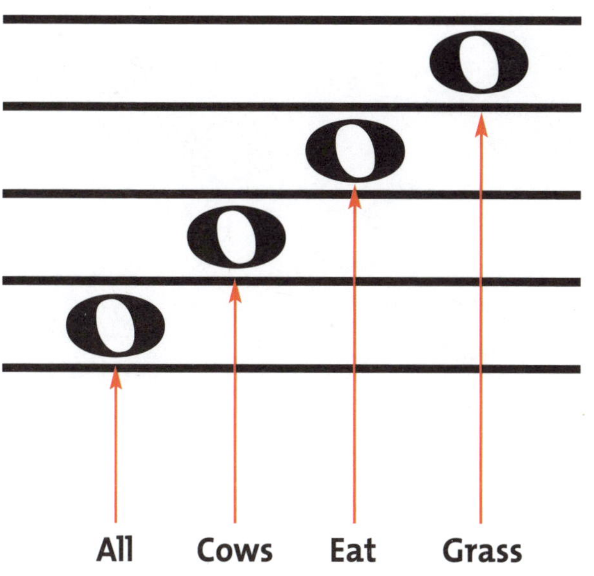
All
Cows
Eat
Grass

Bass Clef Space Notes on Keyboard

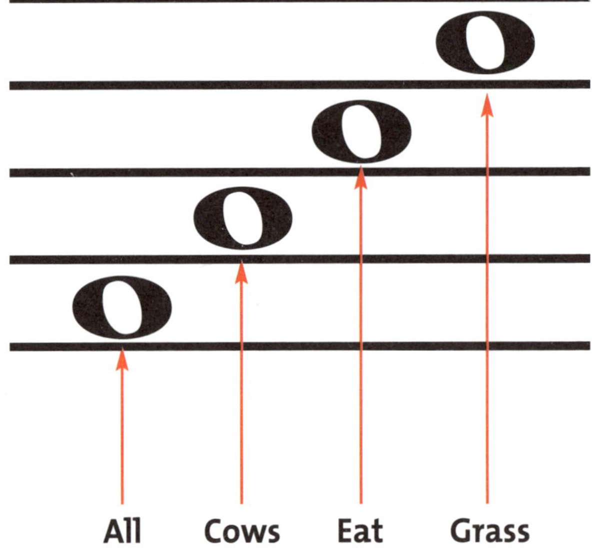

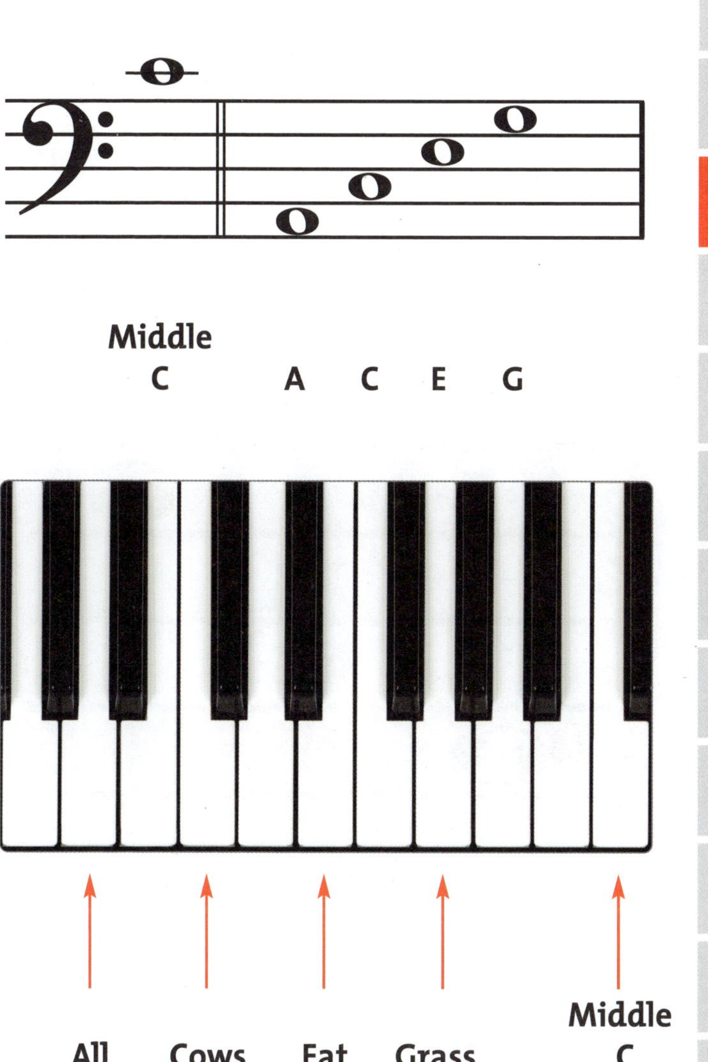
Middle
C
A
C
E
G
All
Cows
Eat
Grass
Middle
C

1
2
3
4
5
6
7
8
9
10
11
12

Bass Clef Space Notes on Guitar

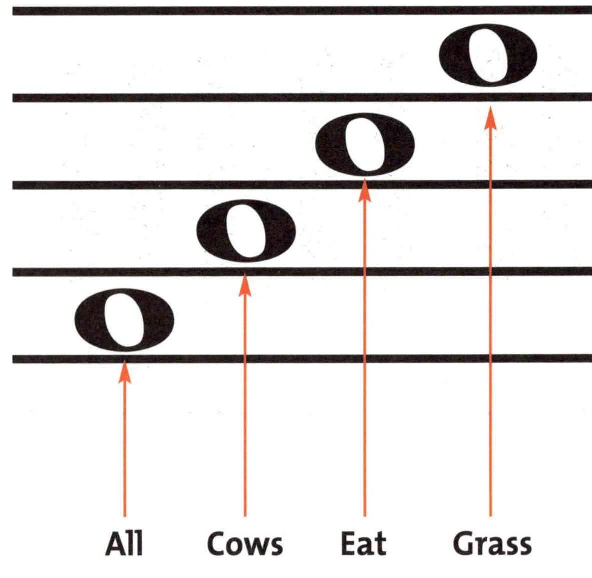

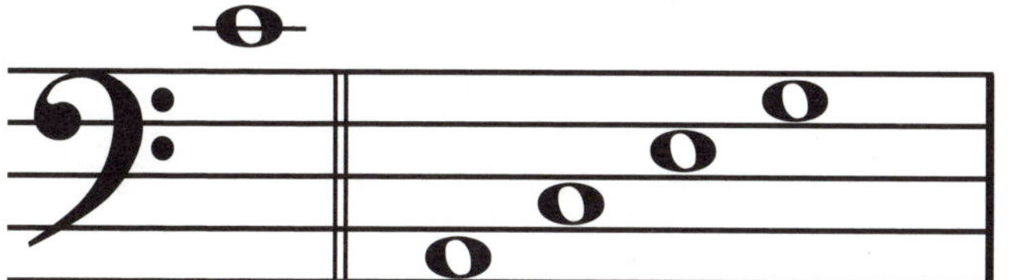

Middle
C A C E G

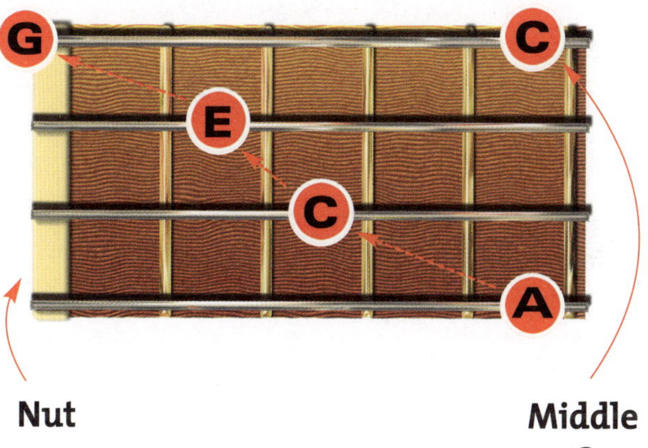

The diagram here is from the player's view. Bass clef line notes on a bass guitar are spread across the strings. The note G is shown on the open string.

1 2 3 4 5 6 7 8 9 10 11 12

Notes Below the Bass Clef Stave

It is very useful to know how to work out the names of the notes below middle C.

Remember that the notes start at the bottom, so the **lower** the **position** of the note on the stave, the **lower** the **note**.

As a guide, a cello would normally only make notes as low as the C two octaves below middle C.

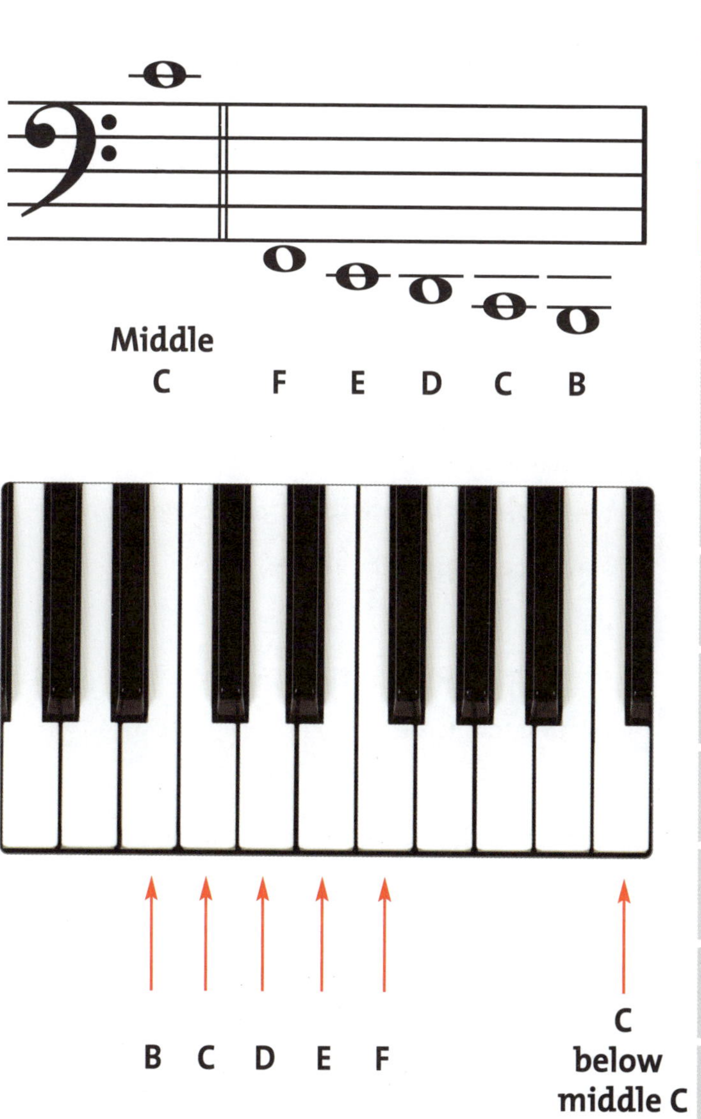
Middle
C
F
E
D
C
B
B
C
D
E
F
C
below
middle C

1
2
3
4
5
6
7
8
9
10
11
12

Notes Above the Bass Clef Stave

It is also useful to know how to work out the names of the notes above the stave.

Remember that the notes start at the bottom, so the **higher** the **position** of the note on the stave, the **higher** the **note**.

The notes **above** the stave can be worked out in relation to middle C.

Remember, the ledger lines only apply where no treble clef is used, or, on the piano, to show that a note should be played with the left hand. The highest note opposite, **G**, is normally the **highest note** played by a double bass or bass guitar.

Middle
C D E F G A

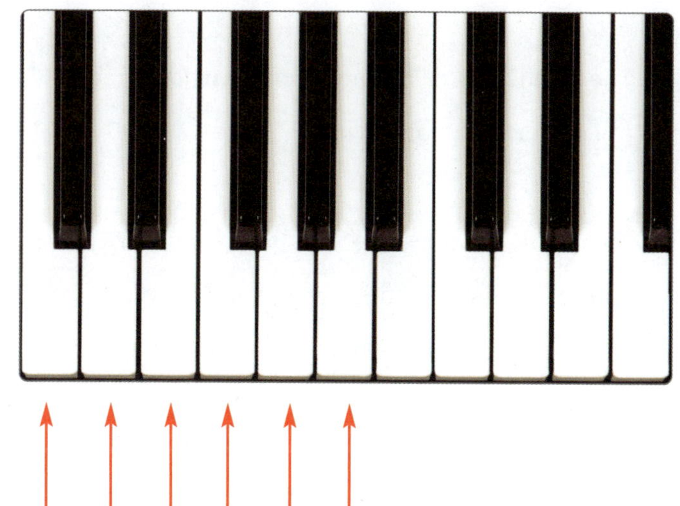

Middle
C D E F G A

1 2 3 4 5 6 7 8 9 10 11 12

4

Notes

Step Four

Notes are the main building blocks of every musical piece.

The **position** of the note on a particular stave tells you which note to play.

The **look** of the note tells you how **long** to sound the note and therefore gives you clues about the pulse of the music and how it relates to the time signature (see page 100).

Notes can be **grouped** together and must be replaced by an equivalent **rest** (see page 88) if no sound is to be played.

Parts of a Note

Notes are made up of four main parts.

1. The **notehead** is either hollow or filled.

2. The **tail** occurs on notes with shorter lengths – quavers and shorter notes.

3. A **beam** is used when connecting notes of the same value. The shorter the length of the note, the greater the number of beams. A semiquaver has two tails, so it has two beams when connected to other semiquavers.

4. A **dot** is used to add half the length of the note. A quaver without a dot is worth two semiquavers. With a dot this increases to three.

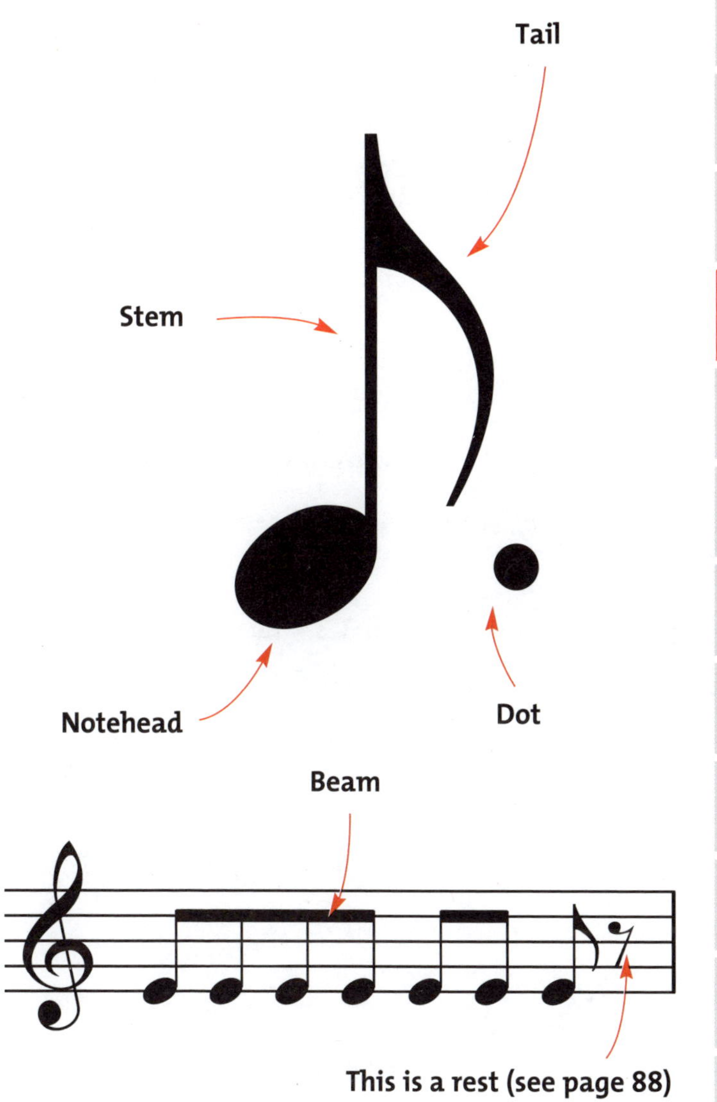
Tail
Stem
Notehead
Dot
Beam
This is a rest (see page 88)

1
2
3
4
5
6
7
8
9
10
11
12

Whole Note/ Semibreve

A semibreve is a note that **fills** the whole bar, hence the alternative name: whole note.

A semibreve has a **hollow notehead**, with no stem, tail, beams or dots.

A semibreve is equal to two minims, four crotchets or eight quavers.

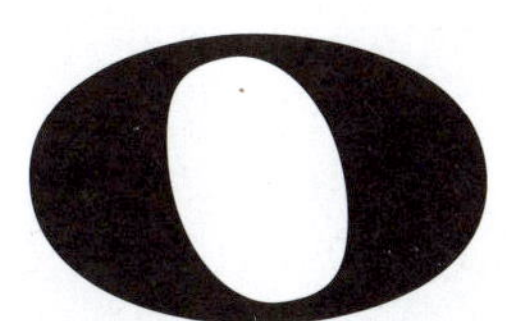

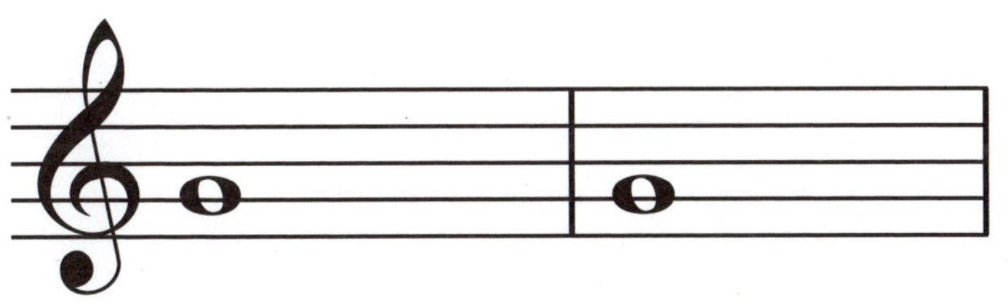

Half Note/ Minim

A minim is a note that fills **half** of a whole bar, hence the alternative name: half note.

A minim has a **hollow notehead** and a stem, but no tail or beams. It can be dotted.

A semibreve is equal to two crotchets, four quavers or eight semiquavers.

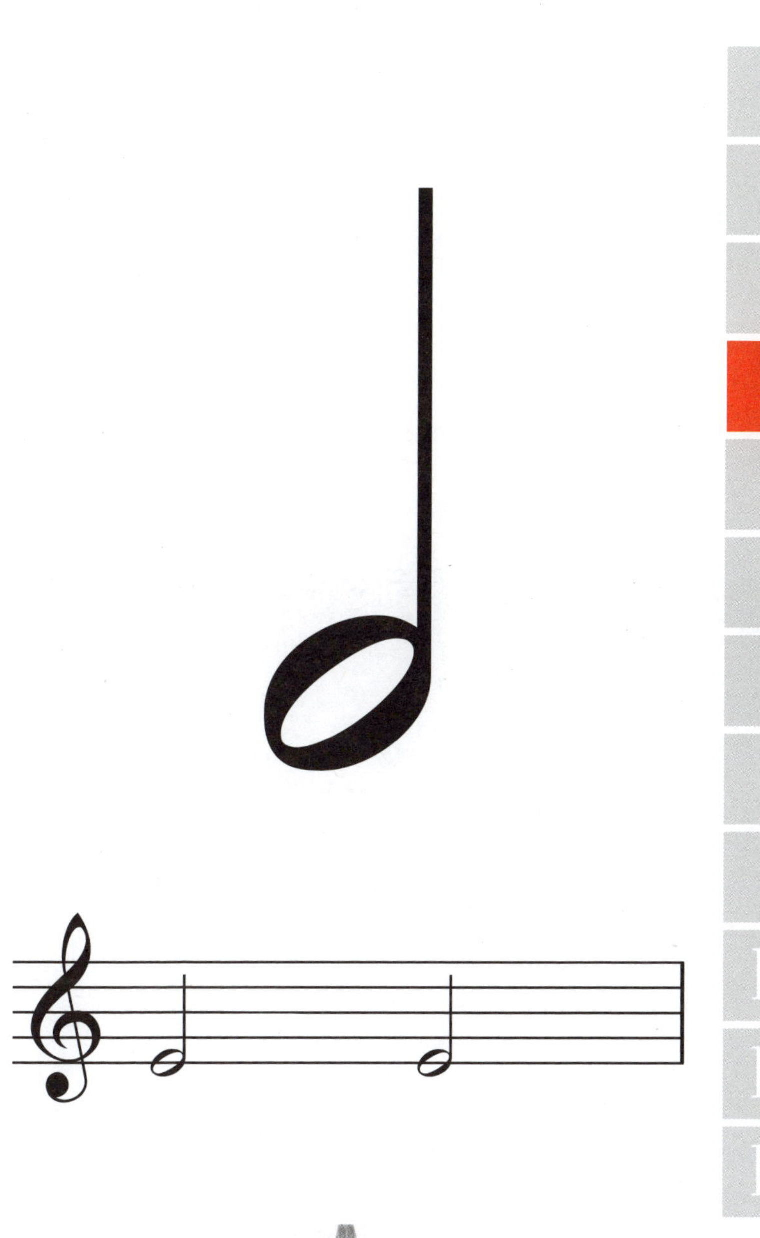

1 2 3 4 5 6 7 8 9 10 11 12

Quarter Note/ Crotchet

A crochet is a note that makes up a **quarter** of the whole bar, hence the alternative name: quarter note.

A crotchet has a **filled-in notehead** and a stem, but no tail or beams. It can be dotted.

A crotchet is equal to half a minim, two quavers or four semiquavers.

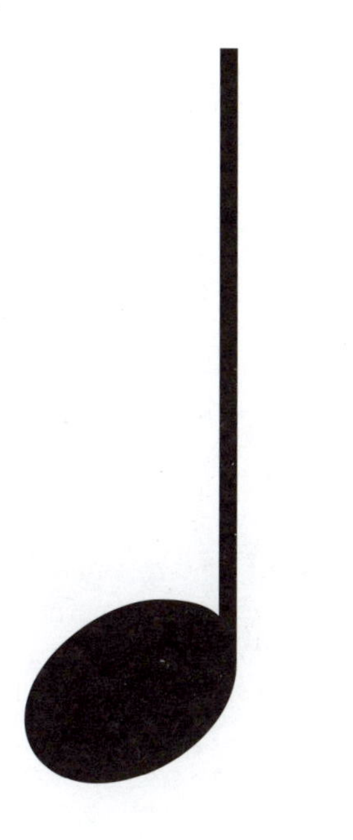

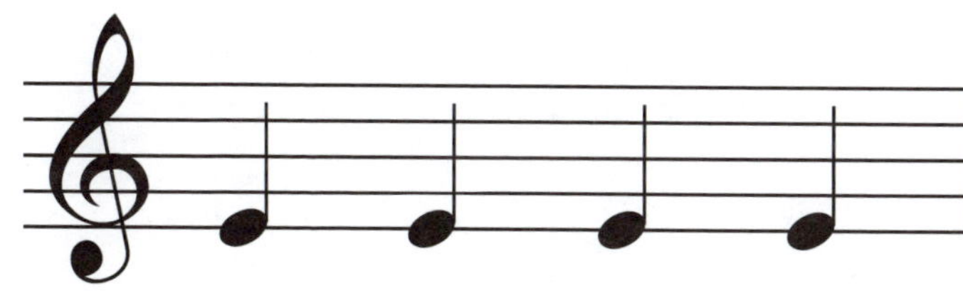

Eighth Note/ Quaver

A quaver is a note that makes up an **eighth** of the whole bar, hence the alternative name: eighth note.

A quaver has a filled-in notehead, a stem, a tail and beams. It can be dotted.

A quaver is equal to two semiquavers.

A single quaver is written with its tail, but quavers are more commonly found in groups with a bar across, to make them easier to read.

This is a quaver rest.

Sixteenth Note/ Semiquaver

A semiquaver is a note that makes up a **sixteenth** of the whole bar, hence the alternative name: sixteenth note.

A semiquaver has a filled-in notehead, a stem and two tails or double beams. It can be dotted.

A semiquaver is equal to two demisemiquavers.

A semiquaver is written with its tails, but they are often found in groups with a beam across, to make them easier to read. The presence of semiquavers usually indicates a fast passage of music.

There are further, shorter notes, with more tails.

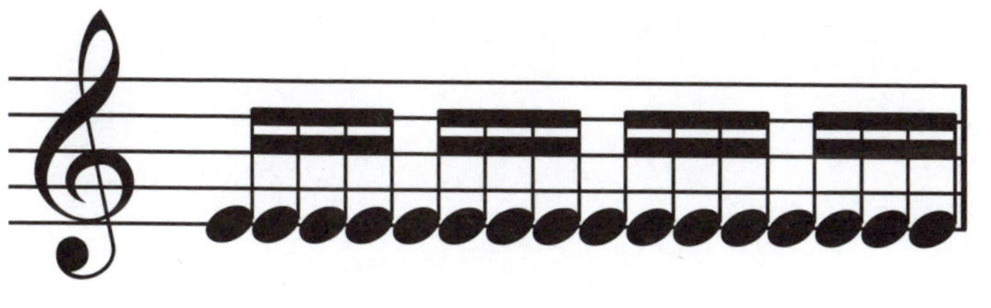

Dotted Notes

The length of the sound of a note can be **increased** by one **half**, by adding a single **dot** to the right-hand side of the notehead.

A **dotted minim** has the same musical length as three crotchets, instead of the usual two, so leaving space for a single crotchet or crotchet rest in the example opposite.

A **dotted crochet** has the same musical length as three quavers. A dotted quaver has the same value as three semiquavers.

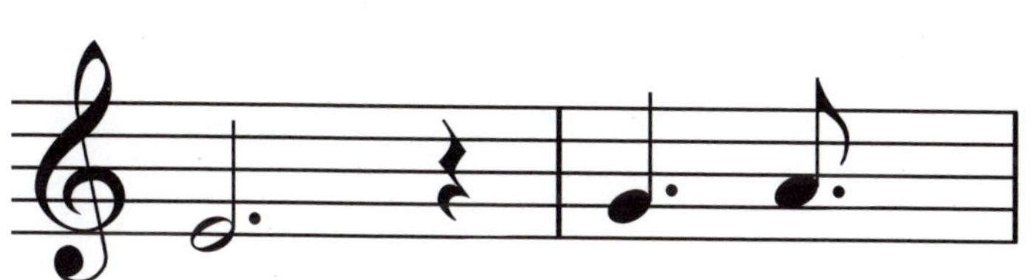

Triplets

Triplets are indicated with a **3** above a group of three notes.

Triplets are three identical notes tied together to fill the space of **two** equivalent notes.

Three **crotchets** grouped as a triplet have the same time value as two crotchets, but **sound faster** because the three notes are played.

Three **quavers** grouped as a triplet have the same time value as two quavers, but sound faster because the three quavers are played.

The triplet of quavers above has the same time value as two quavers below.

Ties

Ties are **curved** lines that connect two notes of the **same pitch**. The line is drawn from notehead to notehead.

Ties are used within a bar to connect two notes where their total value does not have a unique symbol or note. For instance, this is useful for creating the length of a crotchet and a quaver, or a dotted crotchet and a crotchet together.

Ties allow a note to be extended **across** a **bar line**.

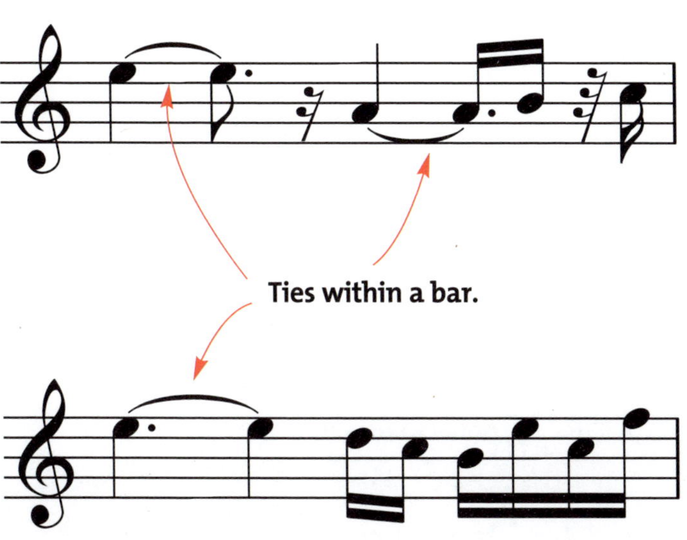
Ties within a bar.

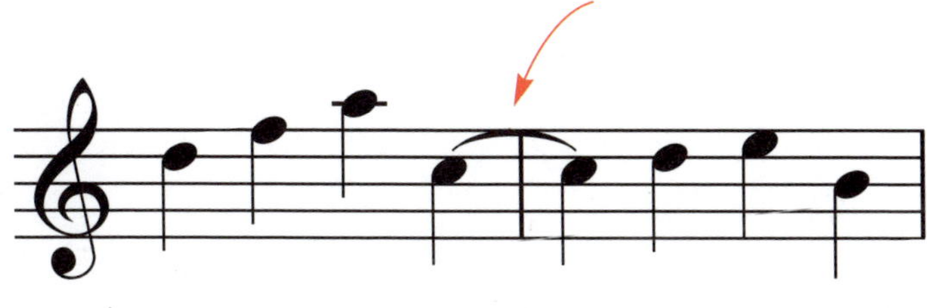
Tie across a bar line.

Slurs

Slurs look like ties but they are not the same.

A slur indicates that the music within the start and end points should be played **smoothly**.

A slur can connect notes of **different** pitches.

A slur can **stretch across** several **bars**.

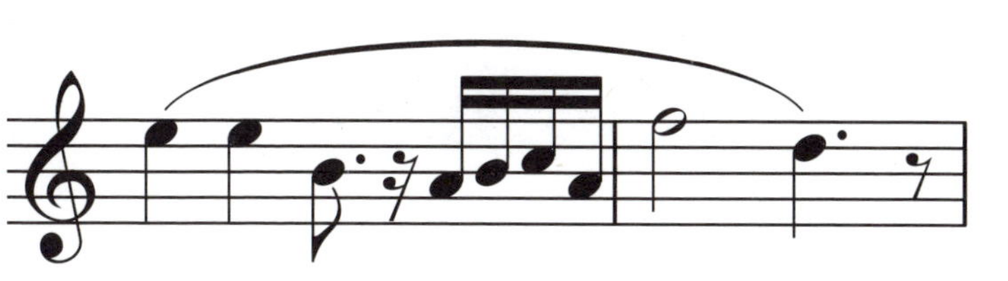

5

The Rests

Step Five

For **every note** there is a corresponding **rest**.

When looking at a bar of music it is important to realize that each bar must **add up** to the number of beats set out at the beginning of the piece. Where no notes are to be played, a rest is put in their place to even out the beats.

The **look** of the rest tells you how **long** to wait.

1 2 3 4 5 6 7 8 9 10 11 12

Whole Note/ Semibreve Rest

The semibreve rest sits under the fourth line from the bottom line of the stave.

The semibreve rest has the same length as a **semibreve** note.

The standard musical bar contains four beats. A semibreve rest lasts for a **whole bar** of four beats.

If a bar only has three beats, the semibreve rest fills the whole bar too.

Note

Rest

Half Note/ Minim Rest

The minim rest sits on top of the third line from the bottom line of the stave.

The minim rest has the same length as a half note, or **minim,** note.

The standard musical bar contains four beats. A minim rest lasts for a **half** a **bar** and so is equal to two beats.

Notes
Rests

1
2
3
4
5
6
7
8
9
10
11
12

Quarter Note/ Crotchet Rest

The crotchet rest is half the length of the minim rest. It has the same length as a quarter note, or **crotchet**.

The standard musical bar contains four beats. A crotchet rest lasts for a **quarter** of a **bar** and so is equal to one beat.

Notes
Rests

Eighth Note/ Quaver Rest

The quaver rest is half the length of the crotchet rest. It has the same length as a eighth note, or **quaver**.

The standard musical bar contains four beats. A quaver rest lasts for an **eighth** of a **bar** and so is equal to half a beat.

1 2 3 4 5 6 7 8 9 10 11 12

Sixteenth Note/ Semiquaver Rest

The semiquaver rest is half the length of the quaver rest. It has the same length as a sixteenth note, or **semiquaver**.

The standard musical bar contains four beats. A semiquaver rest lasts for a **sixteenth** of a **bar** and so has a quarter of a beat.

1 2 3 4 5 6 7 8 9 10 11 12

6

Time Signatures

Step Six

A time signature tells us how many notes and rests will appear in each bar of music.

The time signature determines the **pulse** of the music, whether it will **feel** fast or slow.

Time signatures create the framework around which the notes can be written and understood. They organize the sound to help the listener understand what is happening inside the music.

Two Half Notes Per Bar

The time signature shown with this symbol is **two half notes/minims** for each **bar**.

The **top number** shows that there are **two beats** in every **bar**.

The **bottom** number shows the **length** of each **beat**, in this case **half notes/minims**.

2
2

1 2 3 4 5 6 7 8 9 10 11 12

Two Half Notes Per Bar

The time signature shown with this symbol is an alternative to the symbol on page 103.

The C (which is short for **Cut Time**) means **two half notes/minims** for each **bar**.

There are **two beats** in every **bar**, with each of the two beats being **half notes/minims**.

1
2
3
4
5
6
7
8
9
10
11
12

Two Quarter Notes Per Bar

The time signature shown with this symbol is **two quarter notes/crotchets** for each **bar**.

The **top number** shows that there are **two beats** in every **bar**.

The **bottom** number shows the **length** of each **beat**, in this case **quarter notes/crotchets**.

2
4

Three Quarter Notes Per Bar

The time signature shown with this symbol is **three quarter notes/crotchets** for each **bar**.

The **top number** shows that there are **three beats** in every **bar**.

The **bottom** number shows the **length** of each **beat**, in this case **quarter notes/crotchets**.

3
4

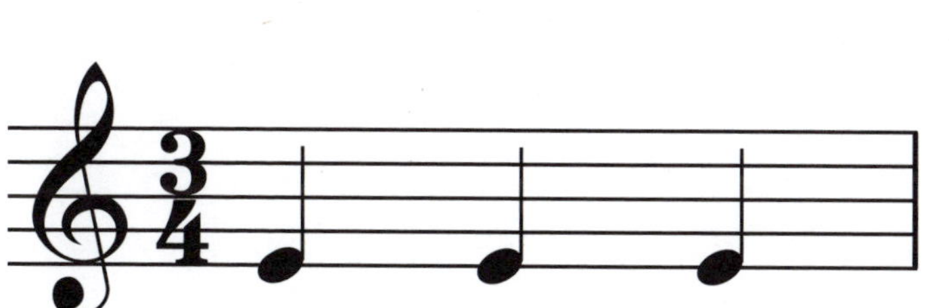

Four Quarter Notes Per Bar

The time signature shown with this symbol is **four quarter notes/crotchets** for each **bar**.

The **top number** shows that there are **four beats** in every **bar**.

The **bottom** number shows the **length** of each **beat**, in this case **quarter notes/crotchets**.

4
4

1 2 3 4 5 6 7 8 9 10 11 12

Four Quarter Notes Per Bar

The time signature shown with this symbol is an alternative to the symbol on the previous page.

The C (which is short for **Common Time**) means **four quarter notes/crotchets** for each **bar**.

There are **four beats** in every **bar**, with each of the four beats being **quarter notes/crotchets**.

1 2 3 4 5 6 7 8 9 10 11 12

Five Quarter Notes Per Bar

The time signature shown with this symbol is **five quarter notes/crotchets** for each **bar**.

The **top number** shows that there are **five beats** in every **bar**.

The **bottom** number shows the **length** of each **beat**, in this case, **quarter notes/crotchets**.

1 2 3 4 5 6 7 8 9 10 11 12

5
4

Six Eighth Notes Per Bar

The time signature shown with this symbol is **six eighth notes/quavers** for each **bar**.

The **top number** shows that there are **six beats** in every **bar**.

The **bottom** number shows the **length** of each **beat**, in this case, **eighth notes/quavers**.

In this time signature the six notes are grouped in threes.

1 2 3 4 5 6 7 8 9 10 11 12

1
2
3
4
5
6
7
8
9
10
11
12

7

Accidentals

Step Seven

The notes we've covered so far in this book have been **natural notes**. They are played on the **white notes** of a piano and have the following names:

A B C D E F G

However, there are notes that sit between some of these whole notes. These are called **accidentals** and on the piano they are played on the **black keys**. These notes are **half** a **tone** (a **semitone**) below or above the **white notes** and are indicated by a **flat**, **sharp** or sometimes a **natural** sign.

Natural & Accidental Notes on the Keyboard

You can see here how the 12 notes work before they are repeated. For clarity at this stage the diagrams opposite just use sharp signs, although later we will look at flat signs too.

On the piano the **natural notes** appear on the **white** keys, with the **sharp** notes on the **black** keys. The difference in pitch between these and any number of notes is called an **interval**.

You can see that black notes do not appear between E and F or B and C. This begins to show us how a **scale**, which depends on different intervals, might work. We look at this later from page 172.

C C♯ D D♯ E F F♯ G G♯ A A♯ B

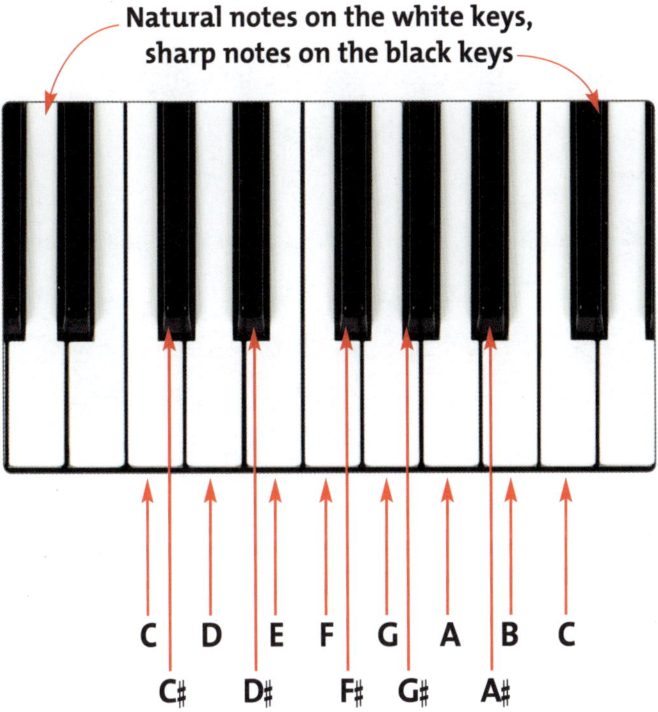

Natural notes on the white keys, sharp notes on the black keys

C D E F G A B C

C♯ D♯ F♯ G♯ A♯

Sharps

This is the **sharp** sign.

It is written to the **left** of a notehead.

A **sharpened** note is half a tone **higher** than the note that is being sharpened.

When a sharp is written in front of a particular note all **subsequent uses** of that note **in the bar** will also be **sharpened**. From the beginning of the **next bar**, the note **reverts** to its previous state.

Sharpened notes are played on the **black** keys of a piano.

Sharp Notes on the Keyboard

Sharp notes appear on the **black** keys on the piano.

Black keys do **not** appear between **every** pair of **white** keys: there is **no black key** between **B** and **C**, or between **E** and **F.**

So **B♯** is the **same note** as **C.**

And **E♯** is the **same note** as **F.**

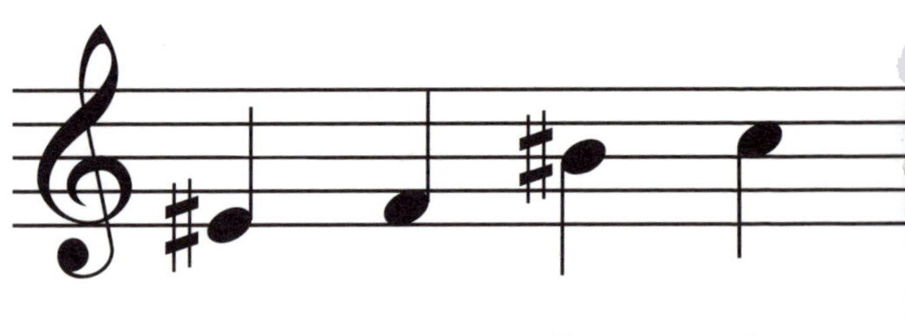

E♯ = F B♯ = C

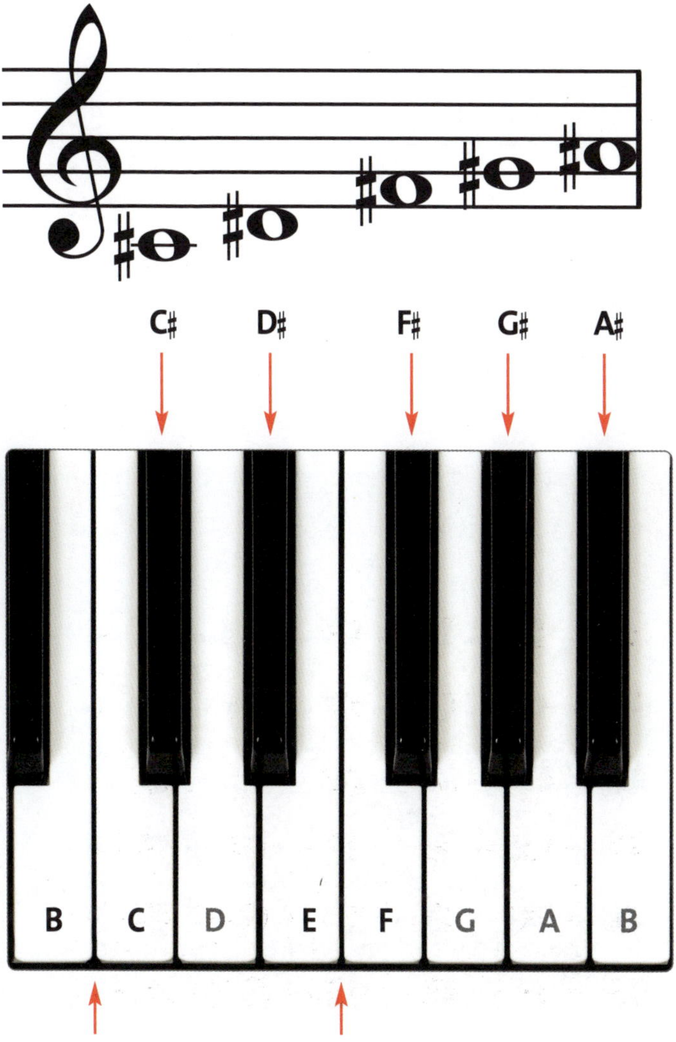

C♯ D♯ F♯ G♯ A♯

B C D E F G A B

Semitone interval between these notes.

1 2 3 4 5 6 7 8 9 10 11 12

Sharp Notes on the Guitar

On the guitar the frets are organized in half tone intervals so **sharp** notes appear after their natural note.

The diagram below shows you all the notes in the **first position** on the guitar.

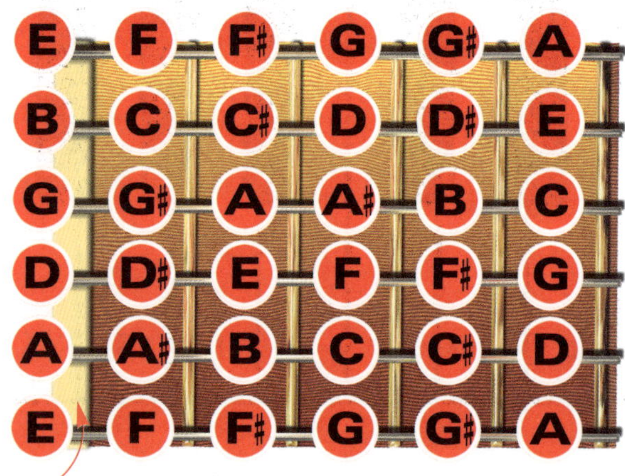

Nut

Player's view. Bass notes at the bottom.

These are the sharp notes in the octave above middle C.

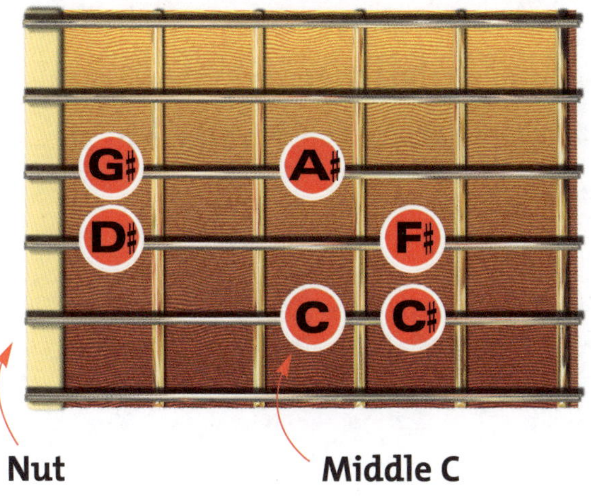

Flats

This is the **flat** sign.

It is written to the **left** of a notehead.

A **flattened** note is half a tone **lower** than the note that is being flattened.

When a flat is written in front of a particular note all **subsequent uses** of that note **in the bar** will also be **flattened**. From the beginning of the **next bar**, the note **reverts** to its previous state.

Flattened notes are played on the **black** keys of a piano.

Flat Notes on the Keyboard

Flat notes appear on the **black** keys on the piano.

As you have seen previously, **black** keys do **not** appear between **every** pair of **white** keys: there is **no black key** between **B** and **C**, or **E** and **F.**

So **C♭** is the **same note** as **B**

And **F♭** is the **same note** as **E.**

F♭ = E C♭ = B

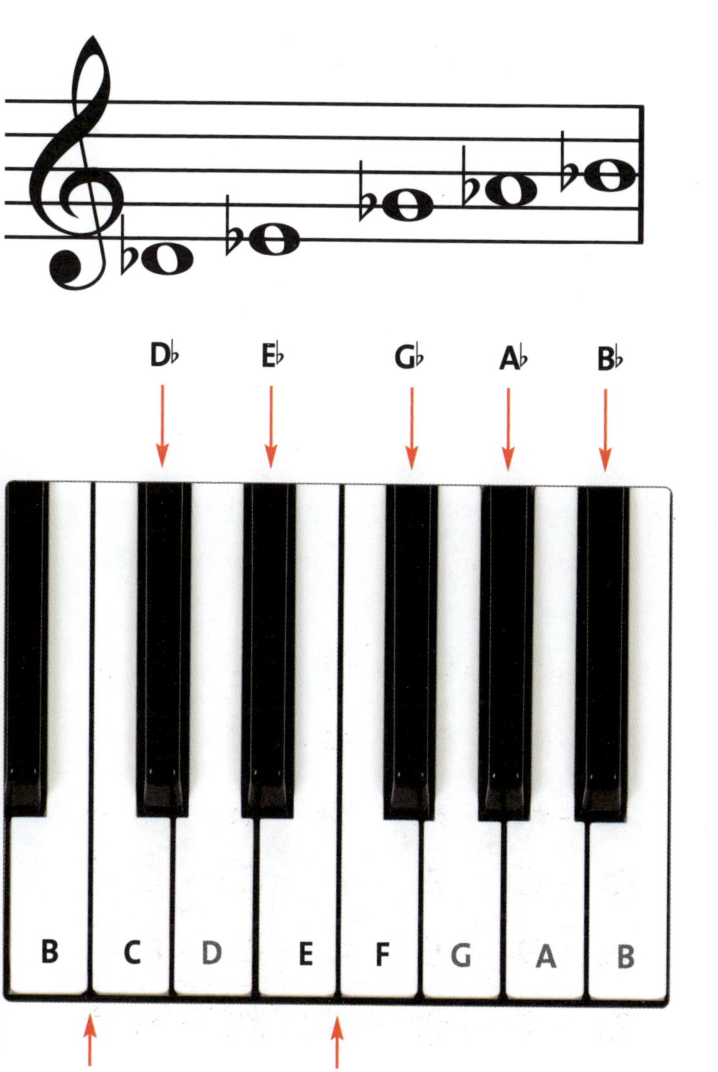

Half note interval between these notes.

1 2 3 4 5 6 7 8 9 10 11 12

Flat Notes on the Guitar

On the guitar the frets are organized in half tone intervals so **flat** notes appear before their natural note.

The diagram below shows you all the notes in the first position on the guitar, using open strings.

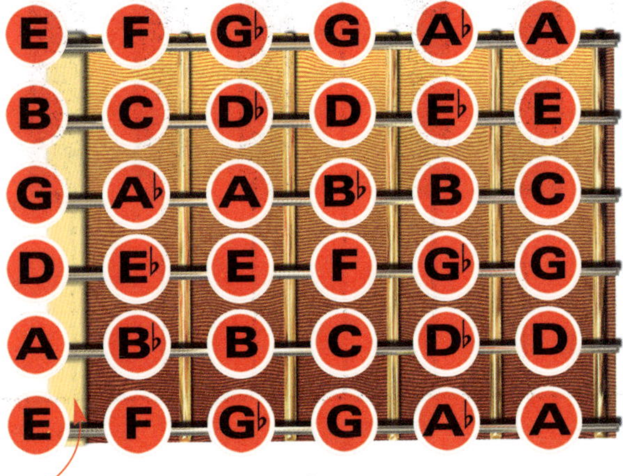

Nut

Players view. Bass notes at the bottom.

These are the flat notes in the octave above middle C.

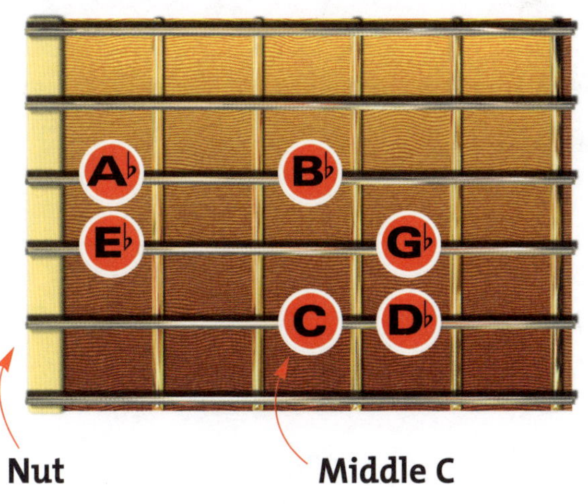

Natural

This is the **natural** sign.

It is written to the **left** of a notehead.

A natural sign is used to **cancel** the effect of a **sharp** or a **flat** note played previously in the same bar, or present in the key signature (see page 140).

Natural notes are played on the **white** keys of a piano.

Natural Notes on the Keyboard

Notes with a **natural** symbol occur when a particular note has been sharpened or flattened previously in the bar or in the key signature.

Once applied, the **natural** symbol for the particular note applies for the rest of bar unless another sharp or flat appears.

A **D♯** is a **semitone** higher than **D♮.**

A **D♭** is a **semitone** lower than **D♮.**

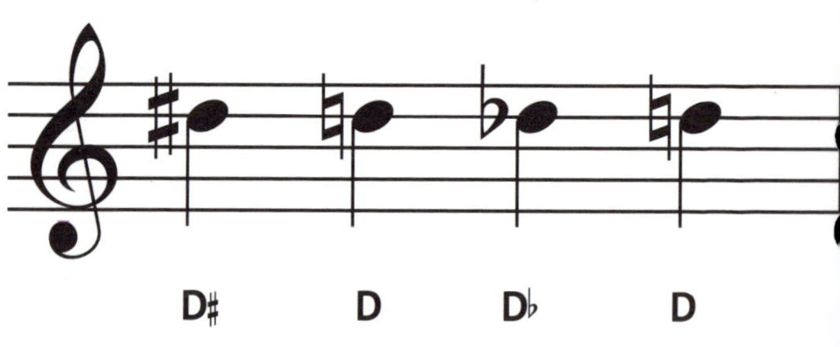

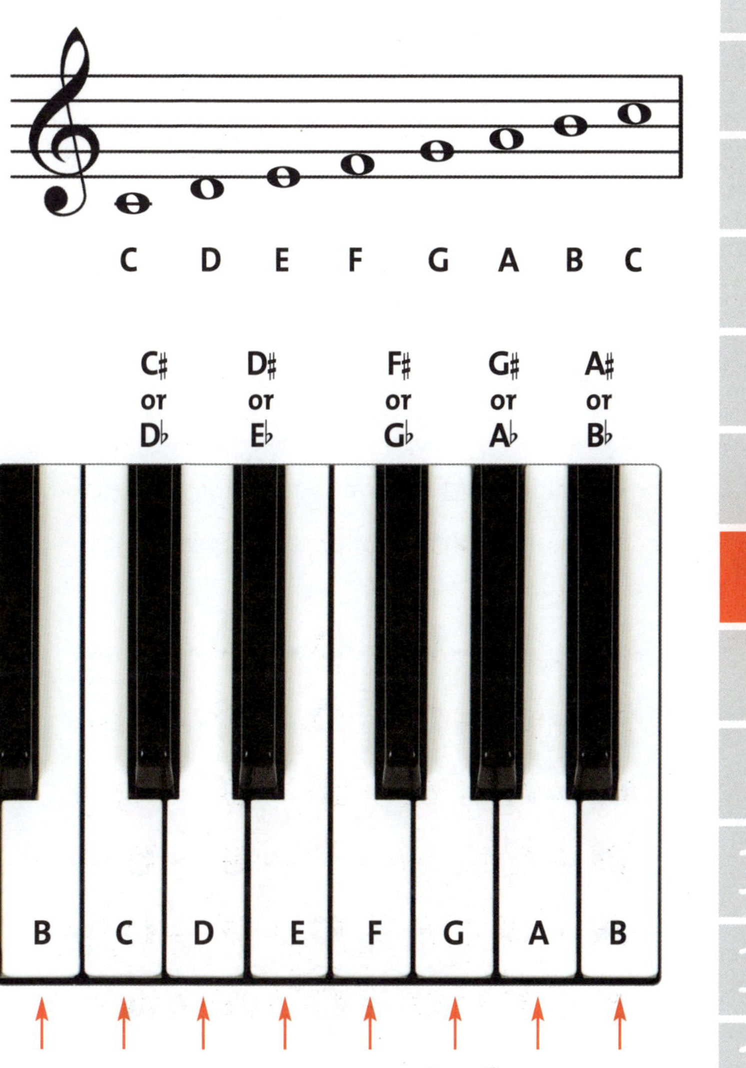

These notes are all **natural**.

Natural Notes on the Guitar

On the guitar the frets are organized in half tone intervals so **flat** notes appear before their natural note and sharps appear after their natural note.

The diagram below shows you all the notes in the first position on the guitar, using open strings.

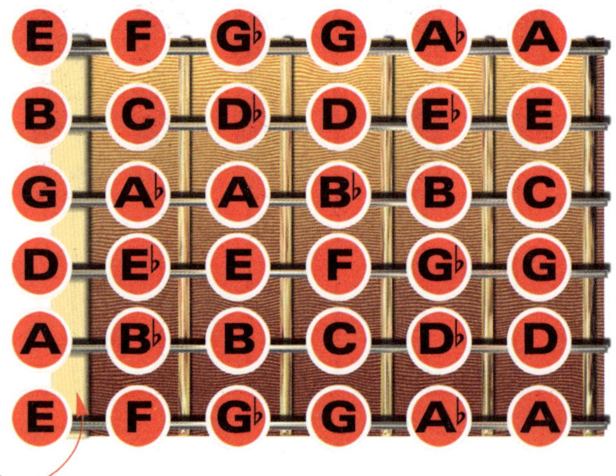

Player's view. Bass notes at the bottom.

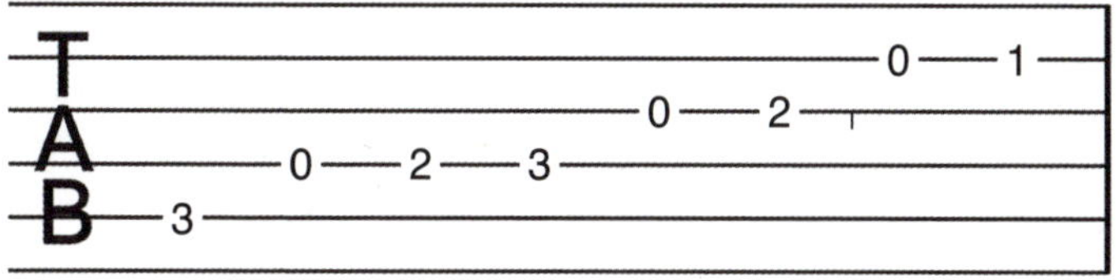

C D E F G A B C

Some guitarists use tablature (called TAB) instead of staff notation. Notes in TAB are shown on six lines representing the six strings of the guitar.

The low E string is at the bottom and the notes are given the fret number on the appropriate string. The natural notes are shown in TAB above and a guitar diagram below.

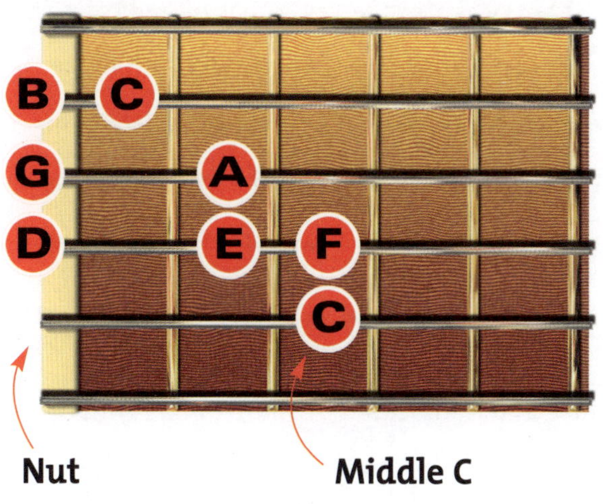

8

Key Signatures

Step Eight

The natural notes above and below **middle C** are the **white** keys on a piano. Key signatures allow us to use the **black** notes, which are the **sharps** and **flats**.

A sharp or flat in the key signature indicates that these accidentals should be played **each time** the note appears. Each key signature contains a different number of either sharps or flats (never both) and makes the music sound distinctive.

A key signature is shown at the **start** of each stave and is indicated by sharp or flat symbols on note lines or spaces.

1 2 3 4 5 6 7 **8** 9 10 11 12

Key Signature

No Sharp or Flat

C Major
A Minor

The keys of C major and its relative, A minor,

have no sharps or flats.

1 2 3 4 5 6 7 8 9 10 11 12

1 2 3 4 5 6 7 8 9 10 11 12

Key Signature

1 Sharp

G Major
E Minor

The keys of G major and its relative, E minor,

have one sharp:

F♯

Key Signature

2 Sharps

D Major
B Minor

The keys of D major and its relative, B minor,

have two sharps:

F♯ C♯

1
2
3
4
5
6
7
8
9
10
11
12

1
2
3
4
5
6
7
8
9
10
11
12

Key Signature

3 Sharps

A Major
F♯ Minor

The keys of A major and its relative, F♯ minor,

have three sharps:

F♯ C♯ G♯

1
2
3
4
5
6
7
8
9
10
11
12

Key Signature

4 Sharps

E Major
C♯ Minor

The keys of E major and its relative, C♯ minor,

have four sharps:

F♯ C♯ G♯ D♯

1 2 3 4 5 6 7 8 9 10 11 12

Key Signature

5 Sharps

B Major
G♯ Minor

The keys of B major and its relative, G♯ minor,

have five sharps:

F♯ C♯ G♯ D♯ A♯

1 2 3 4 5 6 7 8 9 10 11 12

Key Signature

6 Sharps

F♯ Major
D♯ Minor

The keys of F♯ major and its relative, D♯ minor,

have six sharps:

F♯ C♯ G♯ D♯ A♯ E♯

155

1
2
3
4
5
6
7
8
9
10
11
12

Key Signature

7 Sharps

C♯ Major
A♯ Minor

The keys of C♯ major and its relative, A♯ minor,

have seven sharps:

F♯ C♯ G♯ D♯ A♯ E♯ B♯

Key Signature

1 Flat

F Major
D Minor

The keys of F major and its relative, D minor,

have one flat.

1 2 3 4 5 6 7 8 9 10 11 12

Key Signature

2 Flats

B♭ Major
G Minor

The keys of B♭ major and its relative, G minor,

have two flats.

B♭ E♭

1
2
3
4
5
6
7
8
9
10
11
12

Key Signature

3 Flats

E♭ Major
C Minor

The keys of B♭ major and its relative, G minor,

have three flats:

B♭ E♭ A♭

163

1 2 3 4 5 6 7 8 9 10 11 12

Key Signature

4 Flats

A♭ Major
F Minor

The keys of A♭ major and its relative, F minor,

have four flats:

B♭ E♭ A♭ D♭

Key Signature

5 Flats

D♭ Major
B♭ Minor

The keys of D♭ major and its relative, B♭ minor,

have five flats:

B♭ E♭ A♭ D♭ G♭

1
2
3
4
5
6
7
8
9
10
11
12

Key Signature

6 Flats

G♭ Major
E♭ Minor

The keys of G♭ major and its relative, E♭ minor,

have six flats:

B♭ E♭ A♭ D♭ G♭ C♭

169

Key Signature

7 Flats

C♭ Major
A♭ Minor

The keys of C♭ major and its relative, A♭ minor,

have seven flats:

B♭ E♭ A♭ D♭ G♭ C♭ F♭

9

Scales

Step Nine

Scales are rising and falling notes organized according to a particular **pattern**. All key signatures have **major** and **harmonic minor** scales associated with them, but there are other scales that allow further expression and are suitable for different types of music.

In this section we look at six scales per note: **major**, **natural minor**, **harmonic minor**, **melodic minor**, **major pentatonic** and **minor pentatonic**. They each have a distinctive pattern, with the pentatonic scales being particulalry useful for jazz, blues and rock improvisation.

Chromatic Scale

The simplest scale is the chromatic scale because it contains **every note** from the start to the end of an octave. **Every step** of the scale is a **half tone**, or semitone.

Using middle C as the starting point, the C chromatic scale on the keyboard uses **every white** and every **black key** from C to the next C above.

The chromatic scale for every key works in the same way, taking in all the white and black keys, from the starting note of the key to the octave above.

C C♯ D D♯ E F F♯ G G♯ A A♯ B

Piano: right hand fingering C chromatic scale.

C♯/D♭ D♯/E♭ F♯/G♭ G♯/A♭ A♯/B♭

Middle C

2 4 3 2 4

1 3 1 2 1 3 5

C D E F G A B

1 thumb **2** index finger **3** middle finger **4** ring finger **5** little finger

1 2 3 4 5 6 7 8 9 10 11 12

Scale Patterns

The following pages in this section show six scales for each note. Each scale conforms to a standard pattern, from the root note of the scale.

S = semitone (half step); **T** = tone (whole step);
m3 = minor 3rd (three semitones);

Major scale

T T S T T T S

Natural Minor

T S T T S T T

Harmonic Minor

T S T T S m3 S

Melodic Minor

T S T T T T S

(ascending form only)

Major Pentatonic

T T m3 T m3

Minor Pentatonic

m3 T T m3 T

C Major

Scale notes	Up	C D E F G A B C
	down	C B A G F E D C

C Natural Minor

Scale notes	Up	C D E♭ F G A♭ B♭ C
	down	C B♭ A♭ G F E♭ D C

C Harmonic Minor

Scale notes	**Up**	C D E♭ F G A♭ B C
	down	C B A♭ G F E♭ D C

C Melodic Minor

Scale notes	Up	C D E♭ F G A B C
	down	C B♭ A♭ G F E♭ D C

C Major Pentatonic

Scale notes		
	Up	C D E G A C
	down	C A G E D C

C Minor Pentatonic

Scale notes	Up	C E♭ F G B♭ C
	down	C B♭ G F E♭ C

D♭ Major

Scale notes	Up	D♭ E♭ F G♭ A♭ B♭ C D♭
	down	D♭ C B♭ A♭ G♭ F E♭ D♭

C♯ Natural Minor

Scale notes	Up	C♯ D♯ E F♯ G♯ A B C♯
	down	C♯ B A G♯ F♯ E D♯ C♯

C♯ Harmonic Minor

Scale notes

Up	C♯ D♯ E F♯ G♯ A B♯ C♯
down	C♯ B♯ A G♯ F♯ E D♯ C♯

C♯ Melodic Minor

Scale notes	Up	C♯ D♯ E F♯ G♯ A♯ B♯ C♯
	down	C♯ B♮ A♮ G♯ F♯ E D♯ C♯

D♭ Major Pentatonic

Scale notes	Up	D♭ E♭ F A♭ B♭ D♭
	down	D♭ B♭ A♭ F E♭ D♭

C♯ Minor Pentatonic

Scale notes	Up	C♯ E F♯ G♯ B C♯
	down	C♯ B G♯ F♯ E C♯

D Major

Scale notes		
	Up	D E F♯ G A B C♯ D
	down	D C♯ B A G F♯ E D

D Natural Minor

Scale notes	Up	D E F G A B♭ C D
	down	D C B♭ A G F E D

D Harmonic Minor

Scale notes		
	Up	D E F G A B♭ C♯ D
	down	D C♯ B♭ A G F E D

D Melodic Minor

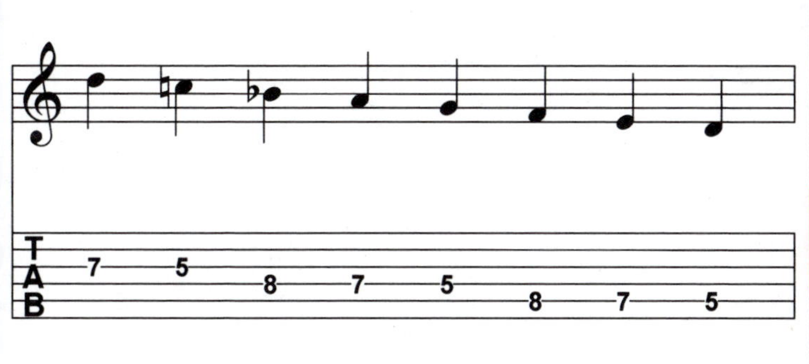

Scale notes	Up	D E F G A B C♯ D
	down	D C♮ B♭ A G F E D

D Major Pentatonic

Scale notes		
	Up	D E F♯ A B D
	down	D B A F♯ E D

D Minor Pentatonic

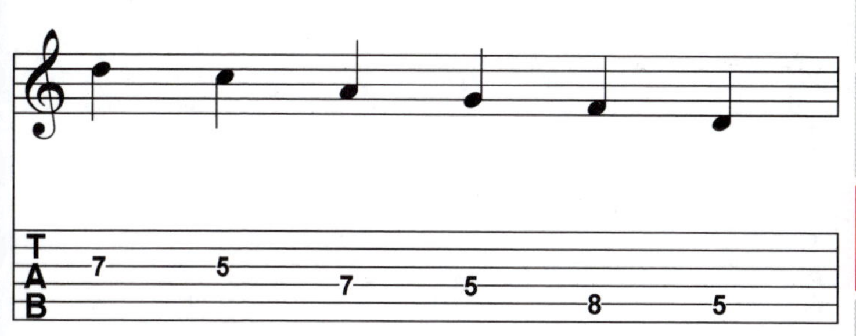

Scale notes	Up	D F G A C D
	down	D C A G F D

1 2 3 4 5 6 7 8 9 10 11 12

E♭ Major

Scale notes	Up	E♭ F G A♭ B♭ C D E♭
	down	E♭ D C B♭ A♭ G F E♭

E♭ Natural Minor

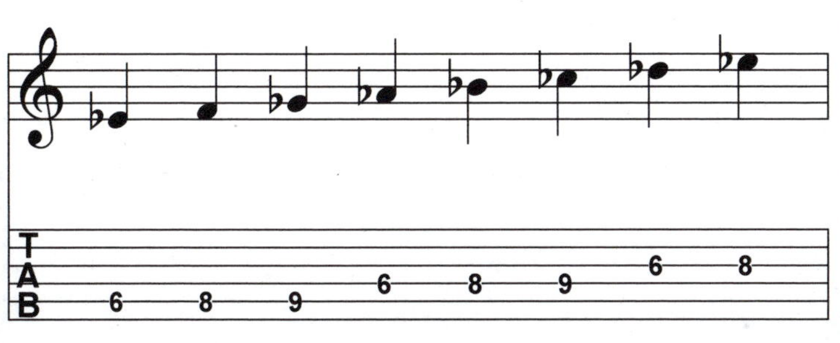

Scale notes

Up	E♭ F G♭ A♭ B♭ C♭ D♭ E♭
down	E♭ D♭ C♭ B♭ A♭ G♭ F E♭

E♭ Harmonic Minor

Scale notes		
	Up	E♭ F G♭ A♭ B♭ C♭ D E♭
	down	E♭ D C♭ B♭ A♭ G♭ F E♭

E♭ Melodic Minor

Scale notes	Up	E♭ F G♭ A♭ B♭ C D E♭
	down	E♭ D♭ C♭ B♭ A♭ G♭ F E♭

1 2 3 4 5 6 7 8 9 10 11 12

E♭ Major Pentatonic

Scale notes	**Up**	E♭ F G B♭ C E♭
	down	E♭ C B♭ G F E♭

E♭ Minor Pentatonic

Scale notes	Up	E♭ G♭ A♭ B♭ D♭ E♭
	down	E♭ D♭ B♭ A♭ G♭ E♭

1 2 3 4 5 6 7 8 **9** 10 11 12

E Major

Scale notes	Up	E F♯ G♯ A B C♯ D♯ E
	down	E D♯ C♯ B A G♯ F♯ E

E Natural Minor

Scale notes	Up	E F♯ G A B C D E
	down	E D C B A G F♯ E

E Harmonic Minor

T
A
B
2 4 5 2 4 5 4 5

Scale notes	Up	E F♯ G A B C D♯ E
	down	E D♯ C B A G F♯ E

E Melodic Minor

Scale notes	Up	E F♯ G A B C♯ D♯ E
	down	E D♮ C♮ B A G F♯ E

E Major Pentatonic

T
A
B
7 9 6 9 6 9

Scale notes

Up	E F♯ G♯ B C♯ E
down	E C♯ B G♯ F♯ E

E Minor Pentatonic

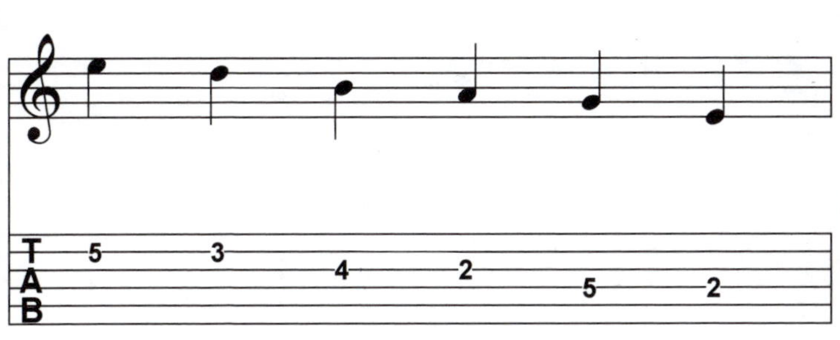

Scale notes	Up	E G A B D E
	down	E D B A G E

F Major

Scale notes	Up	F G A B♭ C D E F
	down	F E D C B♭ A G F

F Natural Minor

Scale notes		
	Up	F G A♭ B♭ C D♭ E♭ F
	down	F E♭ D♭ C B♭ A♭ G F

F Harmonic Minor

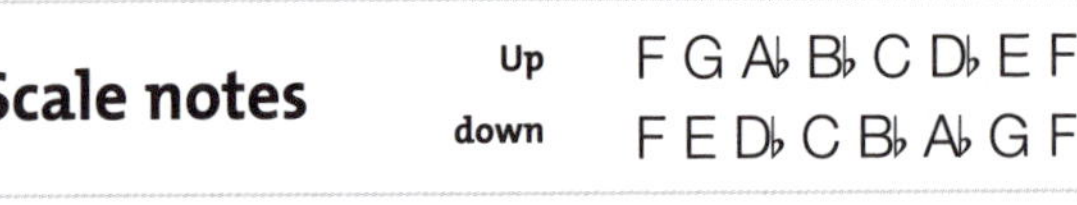

Scale notes

Up	F G A♭ B♭ C D♭ E F
down	F E D♭ C B♭ A♭ G F

F Melodic Minor

Scale notes		
	Up	F G A♭ B♭ C D E F
	down	F E♭ D♭ C B♭ A♭ G F

F Major Pentatonic

T A B 8 5 7 5 7 6

T A B 6 7 5 7 5 8

Scale notes		
	Up	F G A C D F
	down	F D C A G F

F Minor Pentatonic

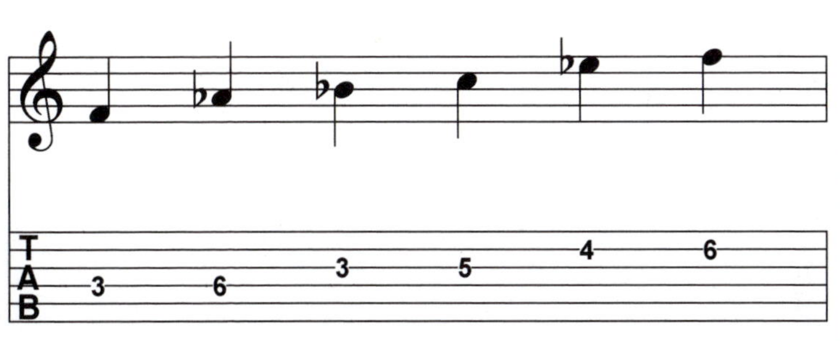

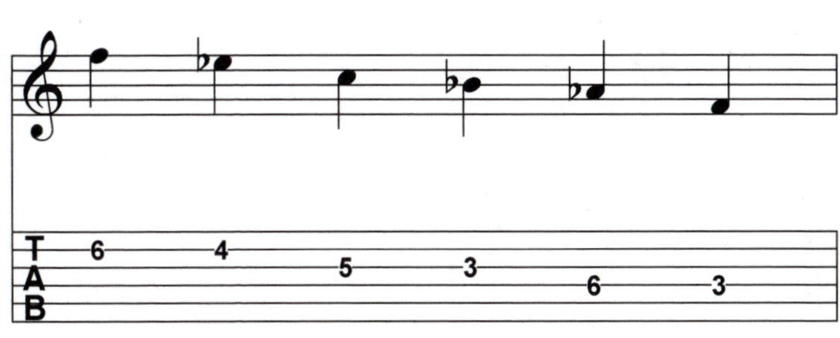

Scale notes

Up	F A♭ B♭ C E♭ F
down	F E♭ C B♭ A♭ F

F♯ Major

Scale notes		
	Up	F♯ G♯ A♯ B C♯ D♯ E♯ F♯
	down	F♯ E♯ D♯ C♯ B A♯ G♯ F♯

F♯ Natural Minor

Scale notes	Up	F♯ G♯ A B C♯ D E F♯
	down	F♯ E D C♯ B A G♯ F♯

F♯ Harmonic Minor

Scale notes	Up	F♯ G♯ A B C♯ D E♯ F♯
	down	F♯ E♯ D C♯ B A G♯ F♯

F♯ Melodic Minor

Scale notes	Up	F♯ G♯ A B C♯ D♯ E♯ F♯
	down	F♯ E♮ D♮ C♯ B A G♯ F♯

F♯ Major Pentatonic

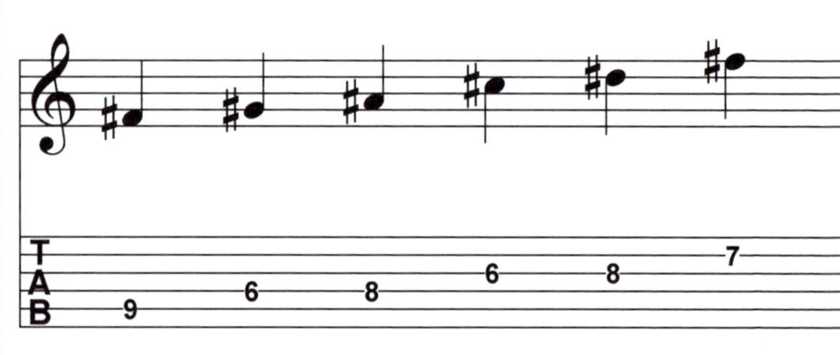

Scale notes	Up	F♯ G♯ A♯ C♯ D♯ F♯
	down	F♯ D♯ C♯ A♯ G♯ F♯

F♯ Minor Pentatonic

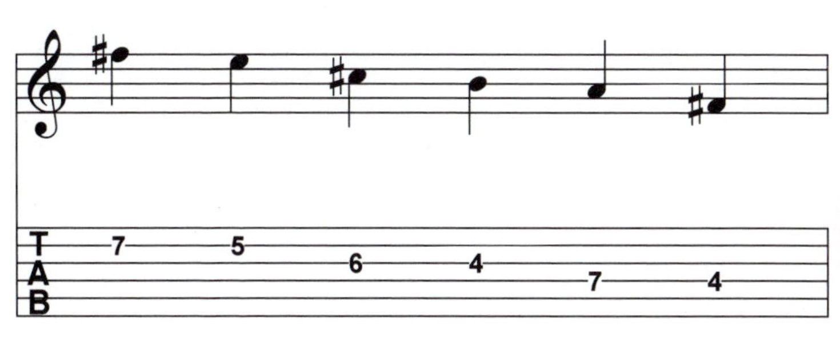

Scale notes	Up	F♯ A B C♯ E F♯
	down	F♯ E C♯ B A F♯

G Major

T
A
B
5 7 4 5 7 5 7 8

Scale notes		
	Up	G A B C D E F♯ G
	down	G F♯ E D C B A G

G Natural Minor

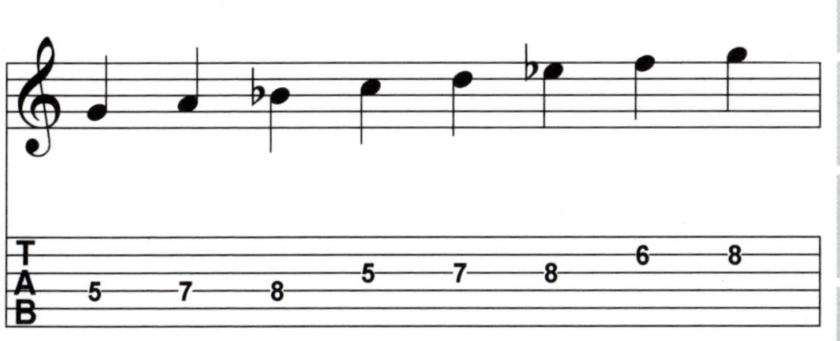

Scale notes	Up	G A B♭ C D E♭ F G
	down	G F E♭ D C B♭ A G

G Harmonic Minor

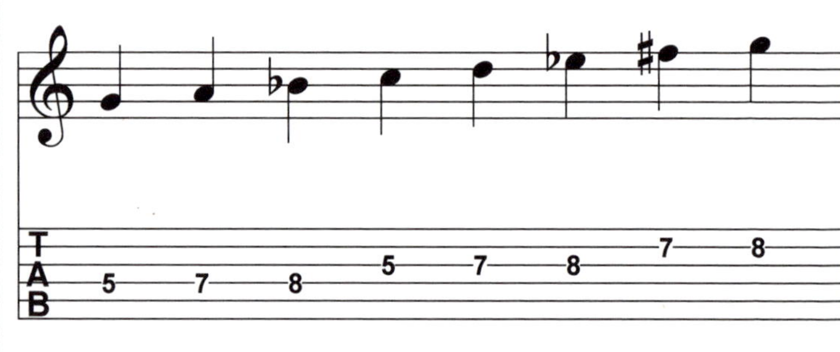

Scale notes		
	Up	G A B♭ C D E♭ F♯ G
	down	G F♯ E♭ D C B♭ A G

G Melodic Minor

Scale notes	Up	G A B♭ C D E F♯ G
	down	G F♮ E♭ D C B♭ A G

G Major Pentatonic

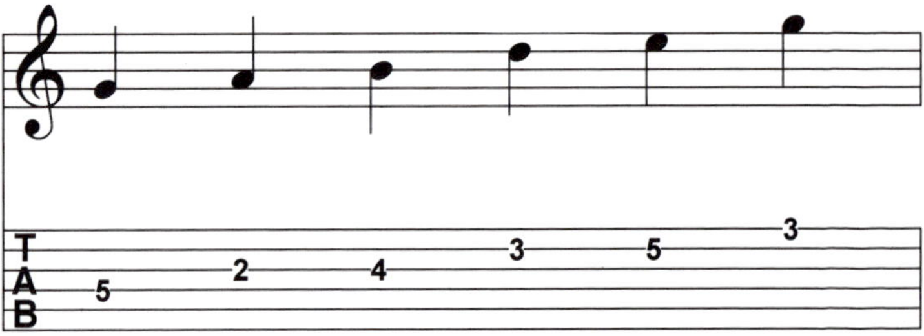

T
A 5 2 4 3 5 3
B

T 3 5 3 4 2 5
A
B

Scale notes	Up	G A B D E G
	down	G E D B A G

G Minor Pentatonic

Scale notes	Up	G B♭ C D F G
	down	G F D C B♭ G

A♭ Major

T
A
B
1 3 1 2 4 1 3 4

Scale notes	Up	A♭ B♭ C D♭ E♭ F G A♭
	down	A♭ G F E♭ D♭ C B♭ A♭

G♯ Natural Minor

Scale notes	Up	G♯ A♯ B C♯ D♯ E F♯ G♯
	down	G♯ F♯ E D♯ C♯ B A♯ G♯

G♯ Harmonic Minor

This double sharp symbol raises the note by two semitones.

Scale notes	Up	G♯ A♯ B C♯ D♯ E F𝄪 G♯
	down	G♯ F𝄪 E D♯ C♯ B A♯ G♯

G♯ Melodic Minor

Scale notes	Up	G♯ A♯ B C♯ D♯ E♯ F𝄪 G♯
	down	G♯ F♯ E♮ D♯ C♯ B A♯ G♯

A♭ Major Pentatonic

TAB 1 3 1 4 1 4

Scale notes	Up	A♭ B♭ C E♭ F A♭
	down	A♭ F E♭ C B♭ A♭

G♯ Minor Pentatonic

Scale notes

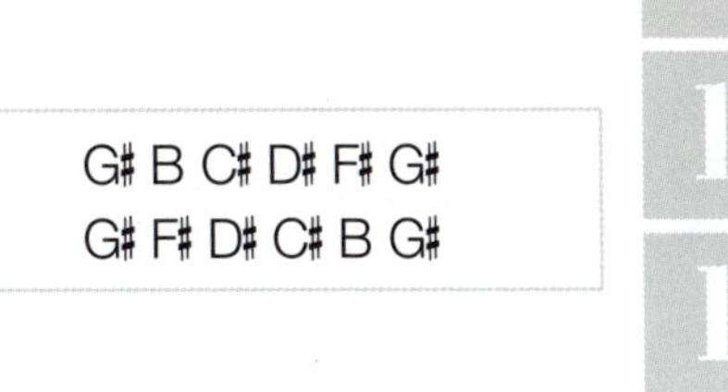

1 2 3 4 5 6 7 8 9 10 11 12

A Major

Scale notes	**Up**	A B C♯ D E F♯ G♯ A
	down	A G♯ F♯ E D C♯ B A

A Natural Minor

Scale notes	Up	A B C D E F G A
	down	A G F E D C B A

1
2
3
4
5
6
7
8
9
10
11
12

A Harmonic Minor

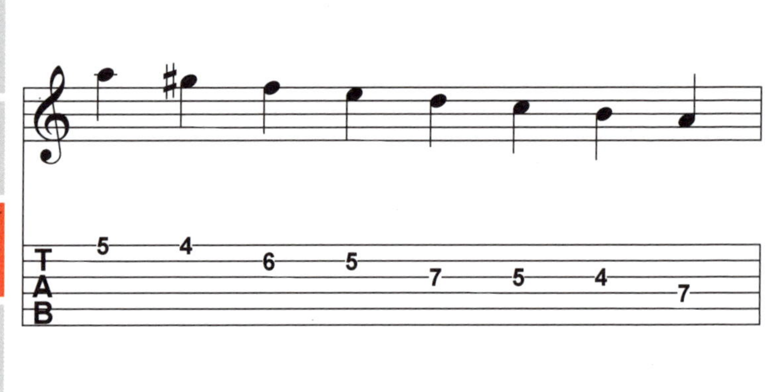

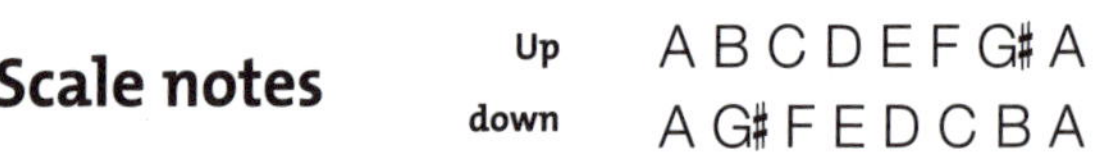

A Melodic Minor

Scale notes		
	Up	A B C D E F♯ G♯ A
	down	A G♮ F♮ E D C B A

1
2
3
4
5
6
7
8
9
10
11
12

A Major Pentatonic

Scale notes	Up	A B C♯ E F♯ A
	down	A F♯ E C♯ B A

A Minor Pentatonic

Scale notes	Up	A C D E G A
	down	A G E D C A

B♭ Major

Scale notes		
	Up	B♭ C D E♭ F G A B♭
	down	B♭ A G F E♭ D C B♭

B♭ Natural Minor

Scale notes	Up	B♭ C D♭ E♭ F G♭ A♭ B♭
	down	B♭ A♭ G♭ F E♭ D♭ C B♭

B♭ Harmonic Minor

TAB
8 5 6 8 6 7 5 6

Scale notes	Up	B♭ C D♭ E♭ F G♭ A B♭
	down	B♭ A G♭ F E♭ D♭ C B♭

B♭ Melodic Minor

Scale notes	Up	B♭ C D♭ E♭ F G A B♭
	down	B♭ A♭ G♭ F E♭ D♭ C B♭

B♭ Major Pentatonic

TAB
3 5 3 6 3 6

TAB
6 3 6 3 5 3

Scale notes	Up	B♭ C D F G B♭
	down	B♭ G F D C B♭

B♭ Major Pentatonic

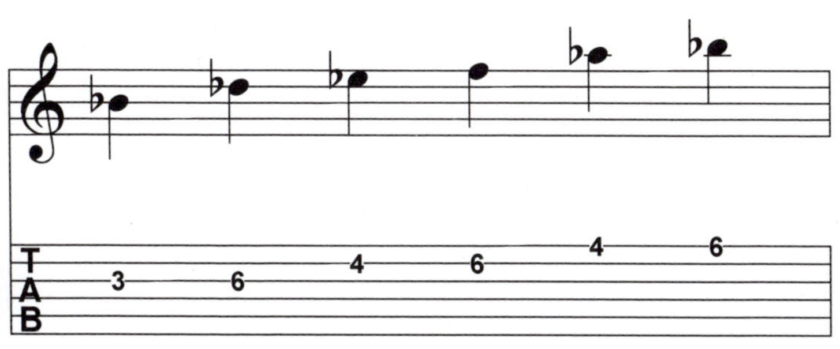

Scale notes	Up	B♭ D♭ E♭ F A♭ B♭
	down	B♭ A♭ F E♭ D♭ B♭

B Major

TAB
4 6 4 5 7 4 6 7

Scale notes		
	Up	B C♯ D♯ E F♯ G♯ A♯ B
	down	B A♯ G♯ F♯ E D♯ C♯ B

B Natural Minor

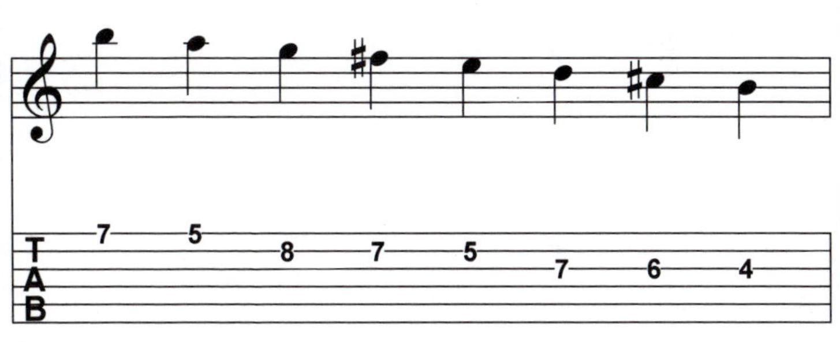

Scale notes	Up	B C♯ D E F♯ G A B
	down	B A G F♯ E D C♯ B

1 2 3 4 5 6 7 8 9 10 11 12

B Harmonic Minor

Scale notes	Up	B C♯ D E F♯ G A♯ B
	down	B A♯ G F♯ E D C♯ B

B Melodic Minor

Scale notes	Up	B C♯ D E F♯ G♯ A♯ B
	down	B A♮ G♮ F♯ E D C♯ B

B Major Pentatonic

Scale notes	Up	B C♯ D♯ F♯ G♯ B
	down	B G♯ F♯ D♯ C♯ B

B Major Pentatonic

Scale notes	Up	B D E F♯ A B
	down	B A F♯ E D B

1
2
3
4
5
6
7
8
9
10
11
12

10

Chords from Scales

Step Ten

We've looked at scales and single notes played one at a time, so now its time to move on to chords, which can be used to **accompany** single-line melodies, or drive choral, band and orchestral writing.

Chords add richness and depth to music and can be played on any instrument capable of making more than one sound at a time: such as keyboard, guitar, or harp. For rock, blues and folk musicians chords often provide the backbone to their songwriting.

Melodic instruments and voices joined together also create a chord-like sound, with many melodies joining in a series of chord-like structures.

How to Make a Chord from a Scale

If you know which **key** to start in, you can **identify** which **chords** will work in that key.

Simple chords are called **triads** because they are made up of **three notes**.

To find the simple triad chords from a scale, use **any note** within to **start**, then **add** the **note two up**, then **add** the note **two up again**.

The **root** note of a chord is the **lowest** note: for example, the C major chord will have C as its root, and D major will have D as its root.

C Major Scale

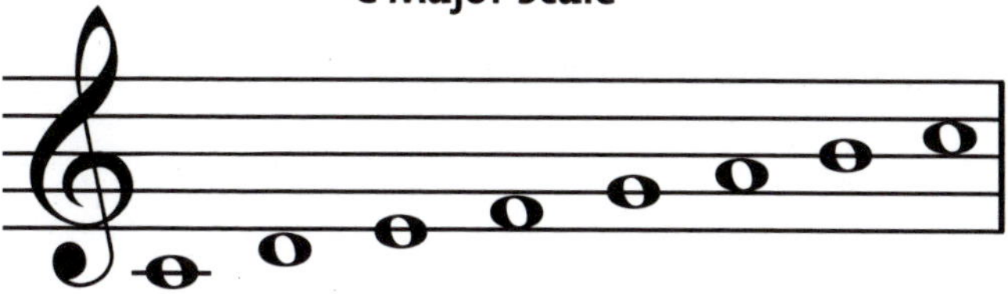

C D E F G A B C

1st 2nd 3rd 4th 5th 6th 7th octave

I II III IV V VI VII

C Major chord

1st + 3rd + 5th notes
of the C Major scale

G
E
C

Root note

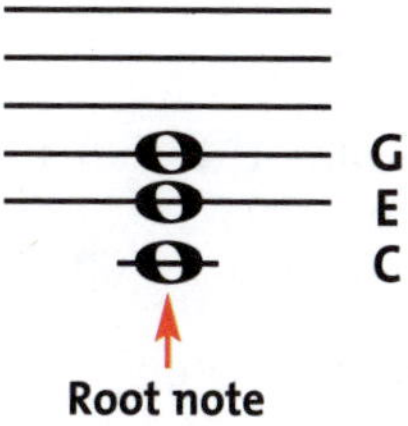

F Major chord

4th + 6th + octave notes
of the C Major scale

C
A
F

Root note

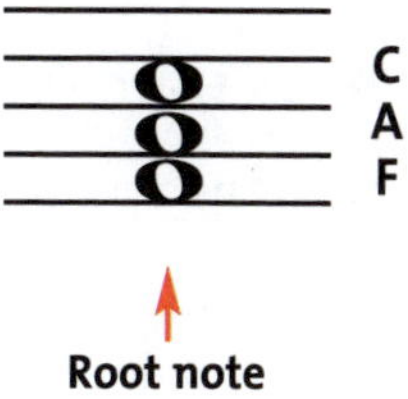

G Major chord

5th + 7th + high 2nd notes
of the C Major scale

D
B
G

Root note

1 2 3 4 5 6 7 8 9 10 11 12

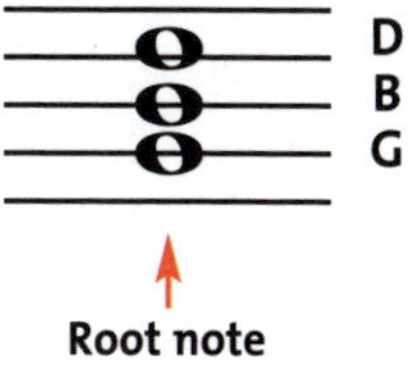

Chord Inversions

A chord that has a bottom note other than its root note is called an **inverted** chord.

Inverted chords are used to add colour and variety to a musical piece. A bass or double bass might play the root notes while the keyboard or string players might play an inverted chord above the root note.

As an example, the C major chord can be played with the root note of C, or the E, or the G.

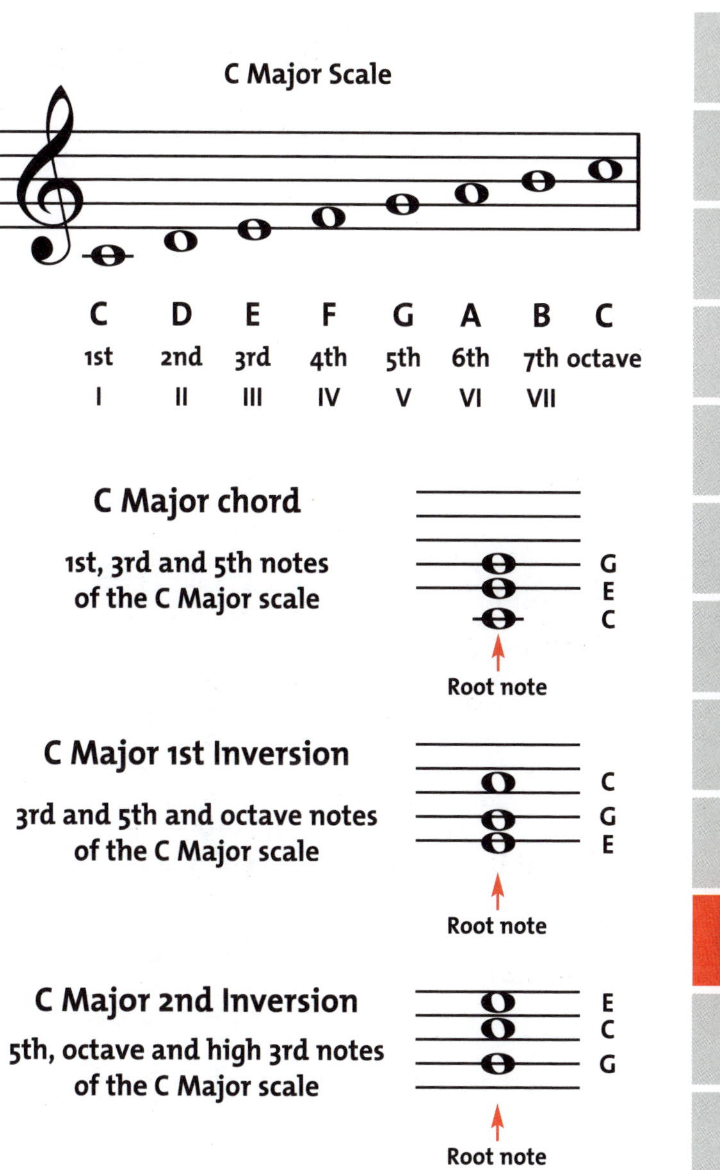
C Major Scale
C D E F G A B C
1st 2nd 3rd 4th 5th 6th 7th octave
I II III IV V VI VII
C Major chord
1st, 3rd and 5th notes of the C Major scale
G
E
C
Root note
C Major 1st Inversion
3rd and 5th and octave notes of the C Major scale
C
G
E
Root note
C Major 2nd Inversion
5th, octave and high 3rd notes of the C Major scale
E
C
G
Root note

Common Chords of the C Major Scale

Notes:	C	D	E	F	G	A	B
	I	II	III	IV	V	VI	VII

Chord I

I, III, V

C Major

Notes: C, E, G

Guitar chord with octaves

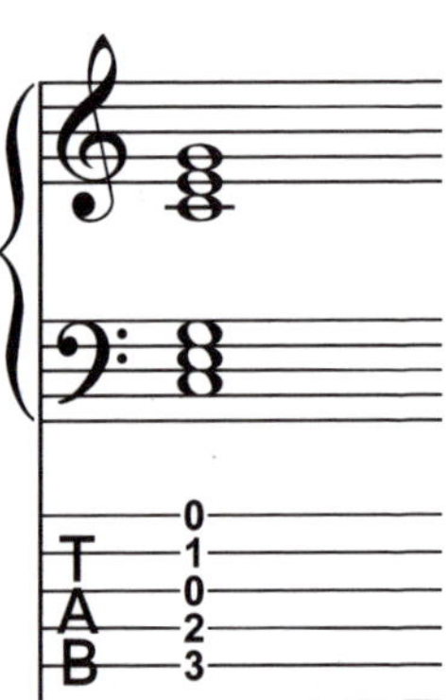

Chord II

II, IV, VI

D Minor

Notes: D, F, A

Guitar chord with octaves

Chord IV

IV, VI, I

F Major

Notes: F, A, C

Guitar chord with octaves

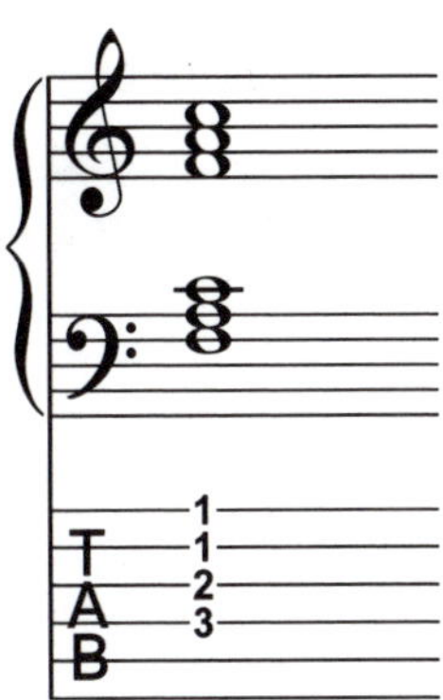

Chord V

V, VII, II

G Major

Notes: G, B, D

Guitar chord with octaves

Chord VI

VI, I, III

A Minor

Notes: A, C, E

Guitar chord with octaves

Common Chords of the D♭ Major Scale

Notes:	D♭	E♭	F	G♭	A♭	B♭	C
	I	II	III	IV	V	VI	VII

Chord I

I, III, V

D♭ Major

Notes: D♭, F, A♭

Guitar chord with octaves

Chord II

II, IV, VI

E♭ Minor

Notes: E♭, G♭, B♭

Guitar chord with octaves

Chord IV

IV, VI, I

G♭ Major

Notes: G♭, B♭, D♭

Guitar chord with octaves

Chord V

V, VII, II

A♭ Major

Notes: A♭, C, E♭

Guitar chord with octaves

Chord VI

VI, I, III

B♭ Minor

Notes: B♭, D♭, F

Guitar chord with octaves

Common Chords of the D Major Scale

Notes:	D	E	F♯	G	A	B	C♯
	I	II	III	IV	V	VI	VII

Chord I

I, III, V

D Major

Notes: D, F♯, A

Guitar chord with octaves

Chord II

II, IV, VI

E Minor

Notes: E, G, B

Guitar chord with octaves

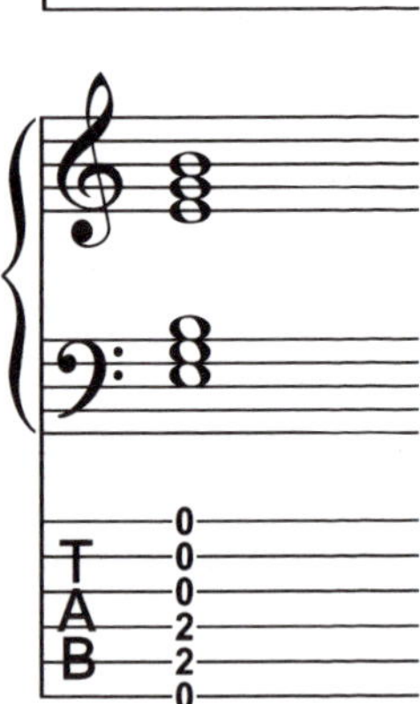

Chord IV

IV, VI, I

G Major

Notes: G, B, D

Guitar chord with octaves

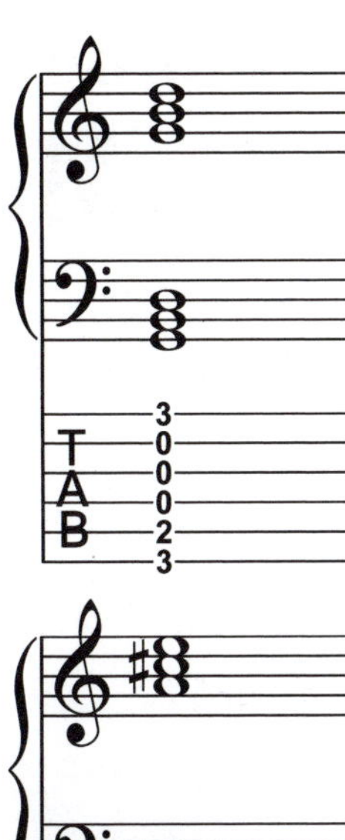

Chord V

V, VII, II

A Major

Notes: A, C♯, E

Guitar chord with octaves

Chord VI

VI, I, III

B Minor

Notes: B, D, F♯

Guitar chord with octaves

Common Chords of the E♭ Major Scale

Notes:	**E♭**	**F**	**G**	**A♭**	**B♭**	**C**	**D**
	I	**II**	**III**	**IV**	**V**	**VI**	**VII**

Chord I

I, III, V

E♭ Major

Notes: E♭, G, B♭

Guitar chord with octaves

Chord II

II, IV, VI

F Minor

Notes: F, A♭, C

Guitar chord with octaves

1 2 3 4 5 6 7 8 9 10 11 12

Chord IV

IV, VI, I

A♭ Major

Notes: A♭, C, E♭

Guitar chord with octaves

Chord V

V, VII, II

B♭ Major

Notes: B♭, D, F

Guitar chord with octaves

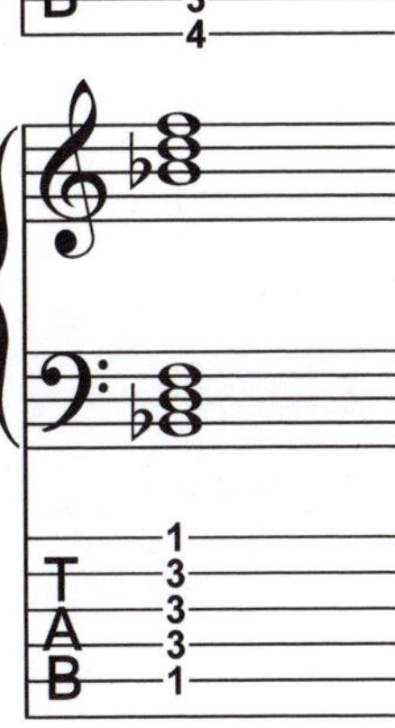

Chord VI

VI, I, III

C Minor

Notes: C, E♭, G

Guitar chord with octaves

Common Chords of the E Major Scale

Notes:	E	F♯	G♯	A	B	C♯	D♯
	I	II	III	IV	V	VI	VII

Chord I

I, III, V

E Major

Notes: E, G♯, B

Guitar chord with octaves

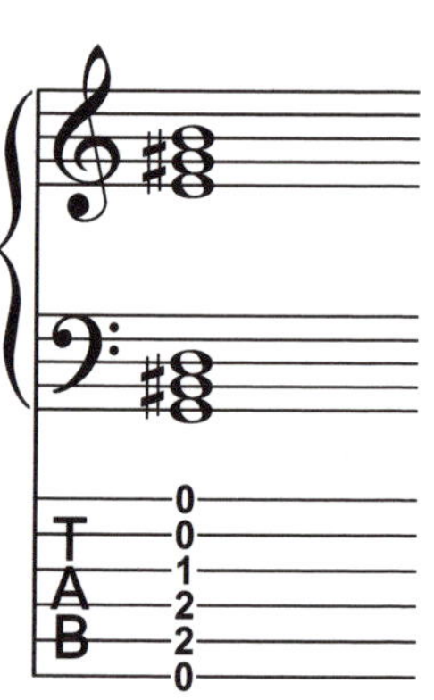

Chord II

II, IV, VI

F♯ Minor

Notes: F♯, A, C♯

Guitar chord with octaves

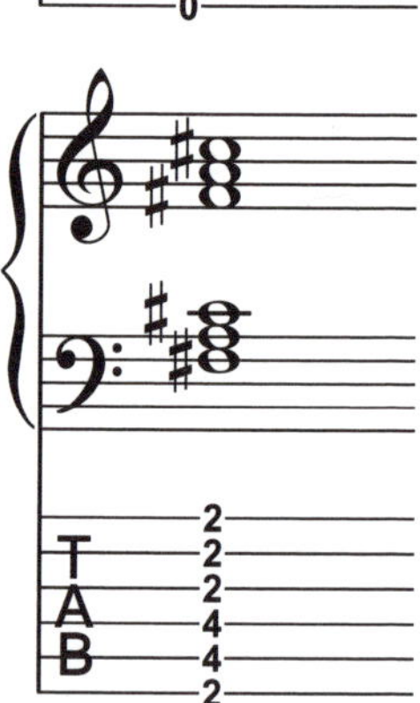

Chord IV

IV, VI, I

A Major

Notes: A, C♯, E

Guitar chord with octaves

Chord V

V, VII, II

B Major

Notes: B, D♯, F♯

Guitar chord with octaves

Chord VI

VI, I, III

C♯ Minor

Notes: C♯, E, G♯

Guitar chord with octaves

Common Chords of the
F Major Scale

Notes:	**F**	**G**	**A**	**B♭**	**C**	**D**	**E**
	I	**II**	**III**	**IV**	**V**	**VI**	**VII**

Chord I

I, III, V

F Major

Notes: F, A, C

Guitar chord with octaves

Chord II

II, IV, VI

G Minor

Notes: G, B♭, D

Guitar chord with octaves

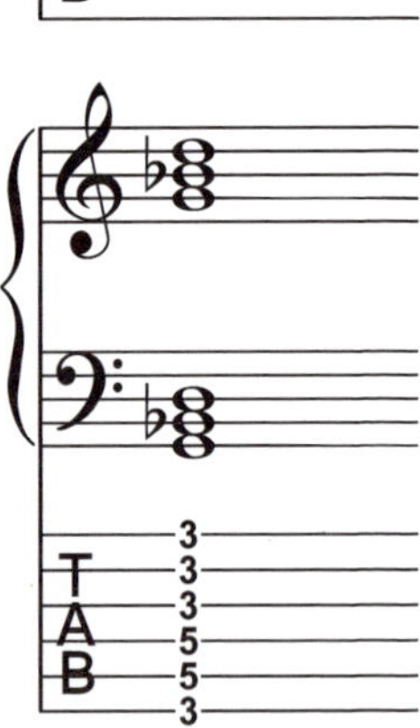

Chord IV

IV, VI, I

B♭ Major

Notes: B♭, D, F

Guitar chord with octaves

Chord V

V, VII, II

C Major

Notes: C, E, G

Guitar chord with octaves

Chord VI

VI, I, III

D Minor

Notes: D, F, A

Guitar chord with octaves

Common Chords of the F♯ Major Scale

Notes:	F♯	G♯	A♯	B	C♯	D♯	E♯
	I	II	III	IV	V	VI	VII

Chord I

I, III, V

F♯ Major

Notes: F♯, A♯, C♯

Guitar chord with octaves

TAB: 2, 2, 3, 4, 4, 2

Chord II

II, IV, VI

G♯ Minor

Notes: G♯, B, D♯

Guitar chord with octaves

Chord IV

IV, VI, I

B Major

Notes: B, D♯, F♯

Guitar chord with octaves

Chord V

V, VII, II

C♯ Major

Notes: C♯, E♯, G♯

Guitar chord with octaves

Chord VI

VI, I, III

D♯ Minor

Notes: D♯, F♯, A♯

Guitar chord with octaves

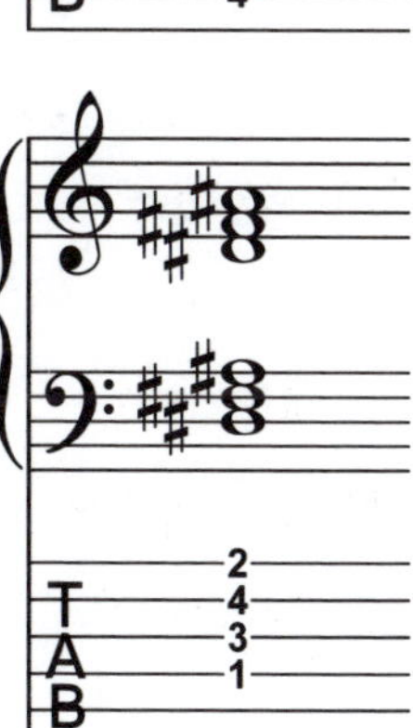

Common Chords of the G Major Scale

Notes:	G	A	B	C	D	E	F♯
	I	II	III	IV	V	VI	VII

Chord I

I, III, V

G Major

Notes: G, B, D

Guitar chord with octaves

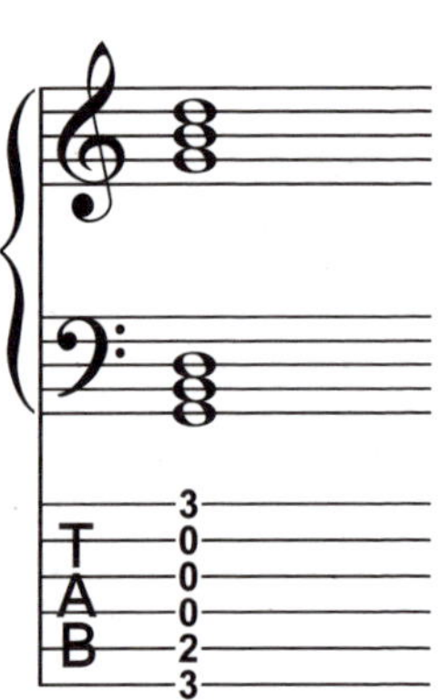

Chord II

II, IV, VI

A Minor

Notes: A, C, E

Guitar chord with octaves

Chord IV

IV, VI, I

C Major

Notes: C, E, G

Guitar chord with octaves

Chord V

V, VII, II

D Major

Notes: D, F♯, A

Guitar chord with octaves

Chord VI

VI, I, III

E Minor

Notes: E, G, B

Guitar chord with octaves

Common Chords of the A♭ Major Scale

Notes:	**A♭**	**B♭**	**C**	**D♭**	**E♭**	**F**	**G**
	I	**II**	**III**	**IV**	**V**	**VI**	**VII**

Chord I

I, III, V

A♭ Major

Notes: A♭, C, E♭

Guitar chord with octaves

Chord II

II, IV, VI

B♭ Minor

Notes: B♭, D♭, F

Guitar chord with octaves

Chord IV

IV, VI, I

D♭ Major

Notes: D♭, F, A♭

Guitar chord with octaves

Chord V

V, VII, II

E♭ Major

Notes: E♭, G, B♭

Guitar chord with octaves

Chord VI

VI, I, III

F Minor

Notes: F, A♭, C

Guitar chord with octaves

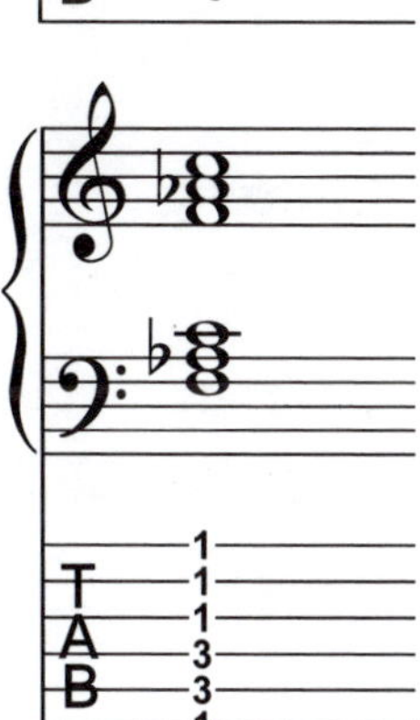

Common Chords of the A Major Scale

Notes:	**A**	**B**	**C♯**	**D**	**E**	**F♯**	**G♯**
	I	**II**	**III**	**IV**	**V**	**VI**	**VII**

Chord I

I, III, V

A Major

Notes: A, C♯, E

Guitar chord with octaves

Chord II

II, IV, VI

B Minor

Notes: B, D, F♯

Guitar chord with octaves

Chord IV

IV, VI, I

D Major

Notes: D, F♯, A

Guitar chord with octaves

Chord V

V, VII, II

E Major

Notes: E, G♯, B

Guitar chord with octaves

Chord VI

VI, I, III

F♯ Minor

Notes: F♯, A, C♯

Guitar chord with octaves

Common Chords of the B♭ Major Scale

Notes:	B♭	C	D	E♭	F	G	A
	I	II	III	IV	V	VI	VII

Chord I

I, III, V

B♭ Major

Notes: B♭, D, F

Guitar chord with octaves

Chord II

II, IV, VI

C Minor

Notes: C, E♭, G

Guitar chord with octaves

Chord IV

IV, VI, I

E♭ Major

Notes: E♭, G, B♭

Guitar chord with octaves

Chord V

V, VII, II

F Major

Notes: F, A, C

Guitar chord with octaves

Chord VI

VI, I, III

G Minor

Notes: G, B♭, D

Guitar chord with octaves

Common Chords of the
B Major Scale

Notes:	B	C♯	D♯	E	F♯	G♯	A♯
	I	II	III	IV	V	VI	VII

Chord I

I, III, V

B Major

Notes: B, D♯, F♯

Guitar chord with octaves

Chord II

II, IV, VI

C♯ Minor

Notes: C♯, E, G♯

Guitar chord with octaves

Chord IV

IV, VI, I

E Major

Notes: E, G♯, B

Guitar chord with octaves

Chord V

V, VII, II

F♯ Major

Notes: F♯, A♯, C♯

Guitar chord with octaves

Chord VI

VI, I, III

G♯ Minor

Notes: G♯, B, D♯

Guitar chord with octaves

1
2
3
4

11
12

11
Chord Sampler
Step Eleven

This section gives a straightforward range chords, for both the guitar and the keyboard or piano.

Major and **minor** chords are given for each key, offering a simple start.

Two other, slightly more complex and interesting chords are also provided: **augmented triads** and **suspended 4ths**. These will help you think about the fingering for your particular instrument and offer a way of **exploring** sounds and scales, particularly when **playing** with **others** or composing and songwriting.

C

Major

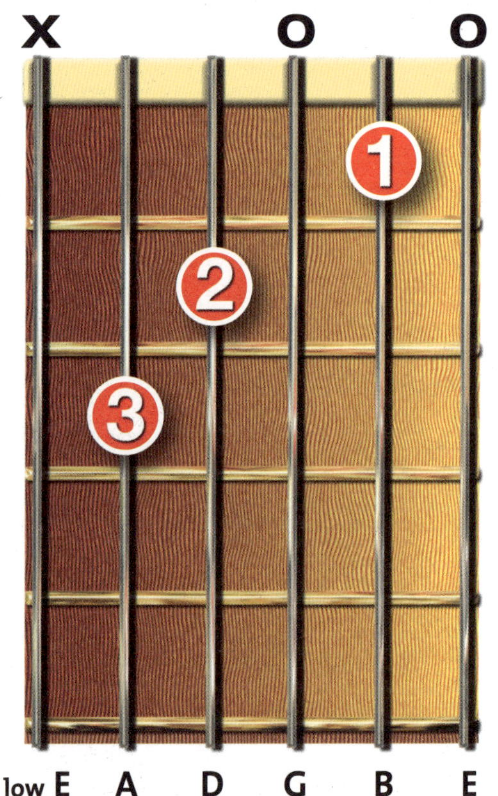

Guitar: first position.

1 index finger **2** middle finger **3** ring finger **4** little finger

Notes of the Chord

1st (C), 3rd (E), 5th (G)

C♯/D♭ D♯/E♭ F♯/G♭ G♯/A♭ A♯/B♭

Middle C

1 3 5

C D E F G A B

Piano: right hand.

1 thumb **2** index finger **3** middle finger **4** ring finger **5** little finger

Cm

Minor

x

3

low E string | A string | D string | G string | B string | E string

Guitar: first position.

1 index finger **2** middle finger **3** ring finger **4** little finger

Notes of the Chord

1st (C), ♭3rd (E♭), 5th (G)

C♯/D♭ D♯/E♭ F♯/G♭ G♯/A♭ A♯/B♭

Middle C

3

1 5

C D E F G A B

Piano: right hand.

1 thumb **2** index finger **3** middle finger **4** ring finger **5** little finger

Csus4

Suspended 4th

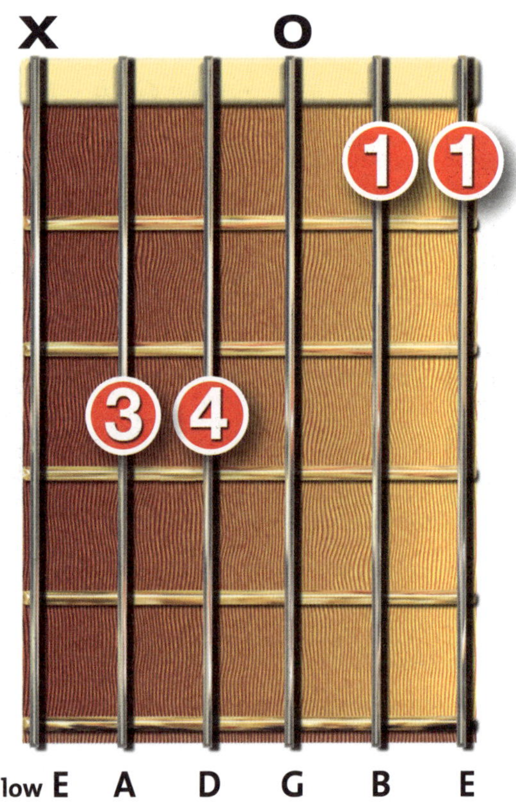

low E string | A string | D string | G string | B string | E string

Guitar: first position.

1 index finger **2** middle finger **3** ring finger **4** little finger

Notes of the Chord

1st (C), 4th (F), 5th (G)

C♯/D♭ D♯/E♭ F♯/G♭ G♯/A♭ A♯/B♭

Middle C

1 4 5

C D E F G A B

Piano: right hand.

1 thumb **2** index finger **3** middle finger **4** ring finger **5** little finger

1 2 3 4 5 6 7 8 9 10 11 12

C+

Augmented

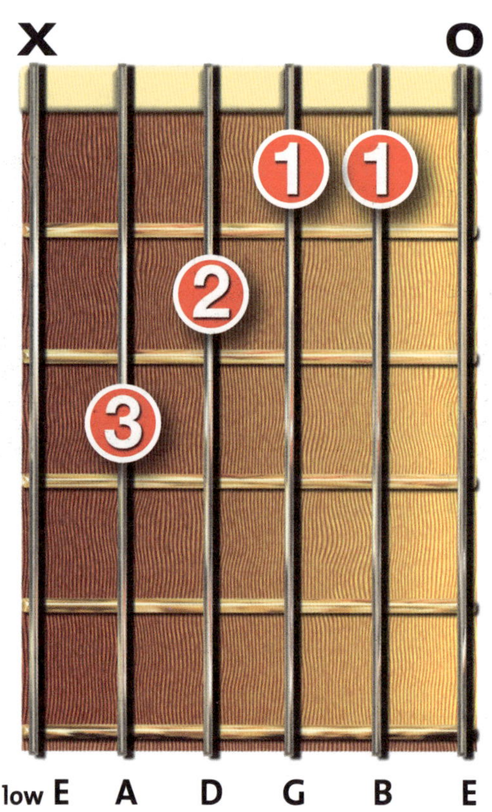

Guitar: first position.

1 index finger **2** middle finger **3** ring finger **4** little finger

Notes of the Chord

1st (C), 3rd (E), ♯5th (G♯)

C♯/D♭ D♯/E♭ F♯/G♭ G♯/A♭ A♯/B♭

Middle C

1 3 5

C D E F G A B

Piano: right hand.

1 thumb **2** index finger **3** middle finger **4** ring finger **5** little finger

C♯/D♭

Major

low **E** string | **A** string | **D** string | **G** string | **B** string | **E** string

Guitar: first position.

1 index finger **2** middle finger **3** ring finger **4** little finger

Notes of the Chord

1st (C♯), 3rd (E♯), 5th (G♯)

C♯/D♭ D♯/E♭ F♯/G♭ G♯/A♭ A♯/B♭

Middle C

1 4 2

C D E F G A B

Piano: right hand.

1 thumb **2** index finger **3** middle finger **4** ring finger **5** little finger

C♯/D♭m

Minor

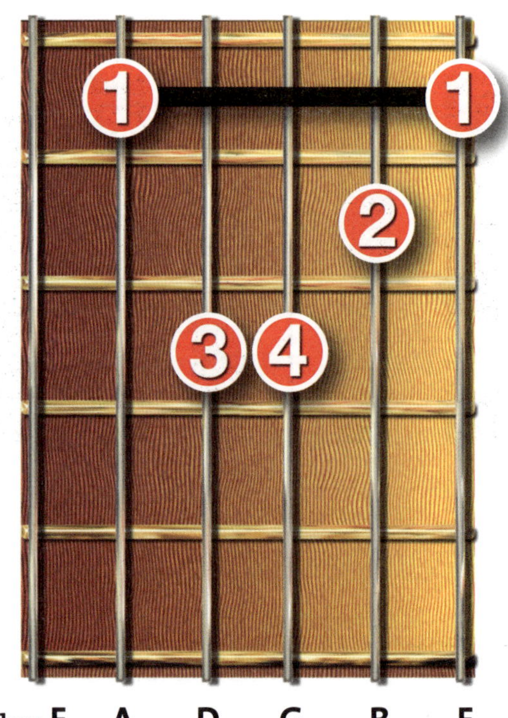

Guitar: first position.

1 index finger **2** middle finger **3** ring finger **4** little finger

Notes of the Chord

1st (C♯), ♭3rd (E), 5th (G♯)

Piano: right hand.

1 thumb **2** index finger **3** middle finger **4** ring finger **5** little finger

1
2
3
4
5
6
7
8
9
10
11
12

C♯sus4/D♭sus4

Suspended 4th

low E string | A string | D string | G string | B string | E string

Guitar: first position.

1 index finger **2** middle finger **3** ring finger **4** little finger

Notes of the Chord

1st (C♯), 4th (F♯), 5th (G♯)

C♯/D♭ D♯/E♭ F♯/G♭ G♯/A♭ A♯/B♭

Middle C

1 2 3

C D E F G A B

Piano: right hand.

1 thumb **2** index finger **3** middle finger **4** ring finger **5** little finger

C♯+/D♭+

Augmented

X X

2

1 1

2

3

low E string A string D string G string B string E string

Guitar: first position.

1 index finger **2** middle finger **3** ring finger **4** little finger

Notes of the Chord

1st (C♯), 3rd (F), ♯5th (Gx)

C♯/D♭ D♯/E♭ F♯/G♭ G♯/A♭ A♯/B♭

Middle C

1 2 4

C D E F G A B

Piano: right hand.

1 thumb **2** index finger **3** middle finger **4** ring finger **5** little finger

D

Major

low E string | **A** string | **D** string | **G** string | **B** string | **E** string

Guitar: first position.

1 index finger **2** middle finger **3** ring finger **4** little finger

Notes of the Chord

1st (D), 3rd (F♯), 5th (A)

C♯/D♭ D♯/E♭ F♯/G♭ G♯/A♭ A♯/B♭

Middle C

2

1 4

C D E F G A B

Piano: right hand.

1 thumb **2** index finger **3** middle finger **4** ring finger **5** little finger

Dm

Minor

low E string | A string | D string | G string | B string | E string

Guitar: first position.

1 index finger **2** middle finger **3** ring finger **4** little finger

Notes of the Chord

1st (D), ♭3rd (F), 5th (A)

C♯/D♭ D♯/E♭ F♯/G♭ G♯/A♭ A♯/B♭

Middle C

1 2 4

C D E F G A B

Piano: right hand.

1 thumb **2** index finger **3** middle finger **4** ring finger **5** little finger

Dsus4

Suspended 4th

X X O

low E string | A string | D string | G string | B string | E string

1 | 3 | 4

Guitar: first position.

1 index finger **2** middle finger **3** ring finger **4** little finger

Notes of the Chord

1st (D), 4th (G), 5th (A)

C♯/D♭ D♯/E♭ F♯/G♭ G♯/A♭ A♯/B♭

Middle C

1 2 3

C D E F G A B

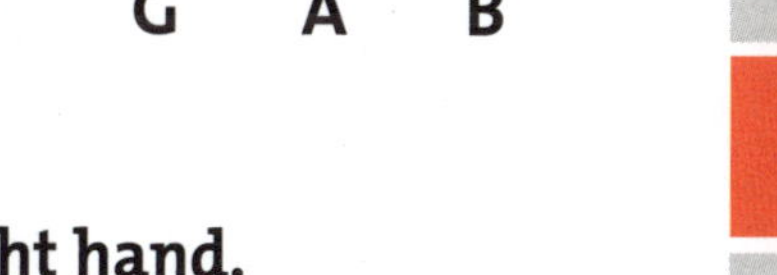

Piano: right hand.

1 thumb **2** index finger **3** middle finger **4** ring finger **5** little finger

D+

Augmented

x x

3

low E string | A string | D string | G string | B string | E string

Guitar: first position.

1 index finger **2** middle finger **3** ring finger **4** little finger

Notes of the Chord

1st (D), 3rd (F♯), ♯5th (A♯)

C♯/D♭ D♯/E♭ F♯/G♭ G♯/A♭ A♯/B♭

Middle C

1 2 4

C D E F G A B

Piano: right hand.

1 thumb **2** index finger **3** middle finger **4** ring finger **5** little finger

D♯/E♭

Major

x

3

low E string | A string | D string | G string | B string | E string

Guitar: first position.

1 index finger **2** middle finger **3** ring finger **4** little finger

Notes of the Chord

1st (E♭), 3rd (G), 5th (B♭)

C♯/D♭ D♯/E♭ F♯/G♭ G♯/A♭ A♯/B♭

Middle C

1 4 2

C D E F G A B

Piano: right hand.

1 thumb **2** index finger **3** middle finger **4** ring finger **5** little finger

D♯m/E♭m

Minor

low E string | A string | D string | G string | B string | E string

Guitar: first position.

1 index finger **2** middle finger **3** ring finger **4** little finger

Notes of the Chord

1st (E♭), ♭3rd (G♭), 5th (B♭)

C♯/D♭ D♯/E♭ F♯/G♭ G♯/A♭ A♯/B♭

Middle C

1 2 4

C D E F G A B

Piano: right hand.

1 thumb **2** index finger **3** middle finger **4** ring finger **5** little finger

1
2
3
4
5
6
7
8
9
10
11
12

D♯sus4/E♭sus4

Suspended 4th

x x

3

low E string | A string | D string | G string | B string | E string

Guitar: first position.

1 index finger **2** middle finger **3** ring finger **4** little finger

Notes of the Chord

1st (E♭), 4th (A♭), 5th (B♭)

C♯/D♭ D♯/E♭ F♯/G♭ G♯/A♭ A♯/B♭

Middle C

1 2 3

C D E F G A B

Piano: right hand.

1 thumb **2** index finger **3** middle finger **4** ring finger **5** little finger

D♯+/E♭+

Augmented

4

low E string | A string | D string | G string | B string | E string

Guitar: first position.

1 index finger **2** middle finger **3** ring finger **4** little finger

Notes of the Chord

1st (E♭), 3rd (G), ♯5th (B)

C♯/D♭ D♯/E♭ F♯/G♭ G♯/A♭ A♯/B♭

Middle C

1 2 4

C D E F G A B

Piano: right hand.

1 thumb **2** index finger **3** middle finger **4** ring finger **5** little finger

E

Major

Guitar: first position.

1 index finger **2** middle finger **3** ring finger **4** little finger

Notes of the Chord

1st (E), 3rd (G♯), 5th (B)

C♯/D♭ D♯/E♭ F♯/G♭ G♯/A♭ A♯/B♭

Middle C

2

1

4

C D E F G A B

Piano: right hand.

1 thumb **2** index finger **3** middle finger **4** ring finger **5** little finger

Em

Minor

low E string | A string | D string | G string | B string | E string

Guitar: first position.

1 index finger **2** middle finger **3** ring finger **4** little finger

Notes of the Chord

1st (E), ♭3rd (G), 5th (B)

C♯/D♭ D♯/E♭ F♯/G♭ G♯/A♭ A♯/B♭

Middle C

1 2 4

C D E F G A B

Piano: right hand.

1 thumb **2** index finger **3** middle finger **4** ring finger **5** little finger

Esus4

Suspended 4th

low E string | A string | D string | G string | B string | E string

Guitar: first position.

1 index finger **2** middle finger **3** ring finger **4** little finger

Notes of the Chord

1st (E), 4th (A), 5th (B)

C♯/D♭ D♯/E♭ F♯/G♭ G♯/A♭ A♯/B♭

Middle C

1 2 3

C D E F G A B

Piano: right hand.

1 thumb **2** index finger **3** middle finger **4** ring finger **5** little finger

1 2 3 4 5 6 7 8 9 10 11 12

E+

Augmented

Guitar: first position.

1 index finger **2** middle finger **3** ring finger **4** little finger

Notes of the Chord

1st (E), 3rd (G♯), ♯5th (B♯)

Piano: right hand.

1 thumb **2** index finger **3** middle finger **4** ring finger **5** little finger

F

Major

low E string	A string	D string	G string	B string	E string

Guitar: first position.

1 index finger **2** middle finger **3** ring finger **4** little finger

Notes of the Chord

1st (F), 3rd (A), 5th (C)

F♯/G♭ G♯/A♭ A♯/B♭ C♯/D♭ D♯/E♭

1 2 4

F G A B C D E

Piano: right hand.

1 thumb **2** index finger **3** middle finger **4** ring finger **5** little finger

1 2 3 4 5 6 7 8 9 10 11 12

Fm

Minor

low E string | A string | D string | G string | B string | E string

Guitar: first position.

1 index finger **2** middle finger **3** ring finger **4** little finger

Notes of the Chord

1st (F), ♭3rd (A♭), 5th (C)

F♯/G♭ G♯/A♭ A♯/B♭ C♯/D♭ D♯/E♭

1 2 4

F G A B C D E

Piano: right hand.

1 thumb **2** index finger **3** middle finger **4** ring finger **5** little finger

Fsus4

Suspended 4th

low E string	A string	D string	G string	B string	E string

Guitar: first position.

1 index finger **2** middle finger **3** ring finger **4** little finger

Notes of the Chord

1st (F), 4th (B♭), 5th (C)

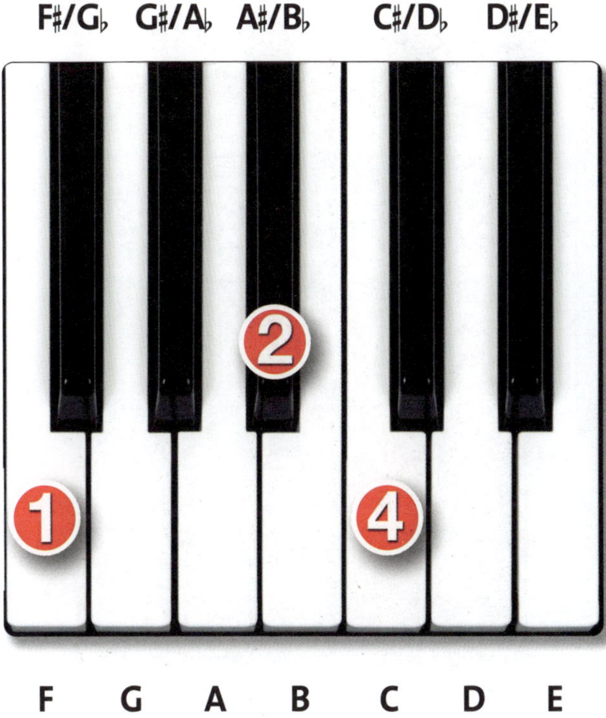
F♯/G♭
G♯/A♭
A♯/B♭
C♯/D♭
D♯/E♭
2
1
4
F
G
A
B
C
D
E

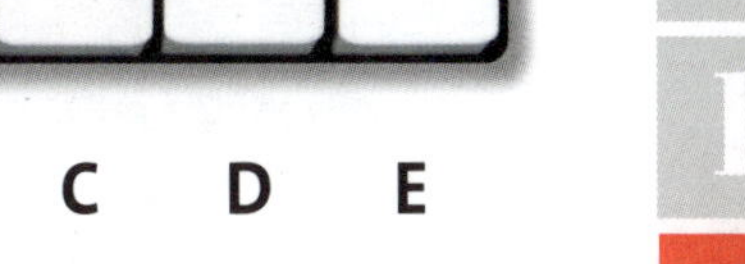

Piano: right hand.

1 thumb **2** index finger **3** middle finger **4** ring finger **5** little finger

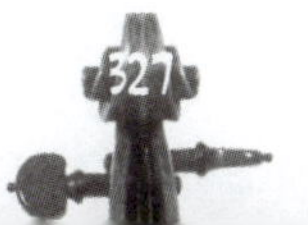

F+

Augmented

low E string | A string | D string | G string | B string | E string

Guitar: first position.

1 index finger **2** middle finger **3** ring finger **4** little finger

Notes of the Chord

1st (F), 3rd (A), ♯5th (C♯)

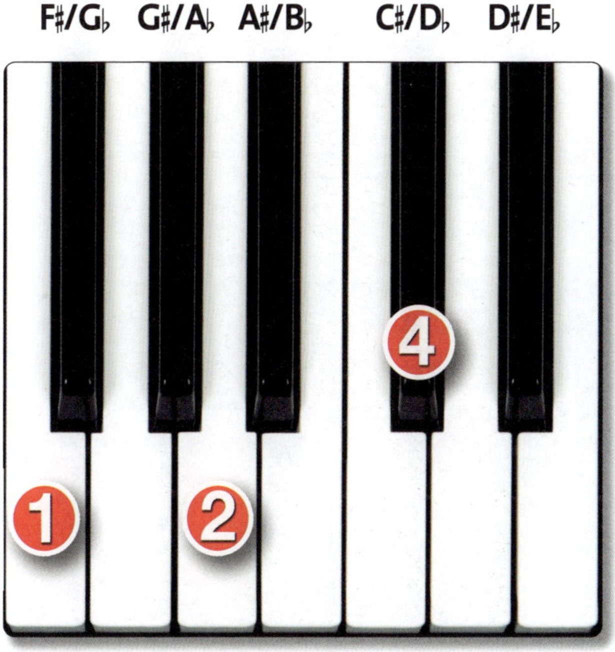

F♯/G♭ G♯/A♭ A♯/B♭ C♯/D♭ D♯/E♭

1 2 4

F G A B C D E

Piano: right hand.

1 thumb **2** index finger **3** middle finger **4** ring finger **5** little finger

F♯/G♭

Major

low E string | A string | D string | G string | B string | E string

Guitar: first position.

1 index finger **2** middle finger **3** ring finger **4** little finger

Notes of the Chord

1st (F♯), 3rd (A♯), 5th (C♯)

Piano: right hand.

1 thumb **2** index finger **3** middle finger **4** ring finger **5** little finger

F♯m/G♭m

Minor

1
2
3
4
5
6
7
8
9
10
11
12

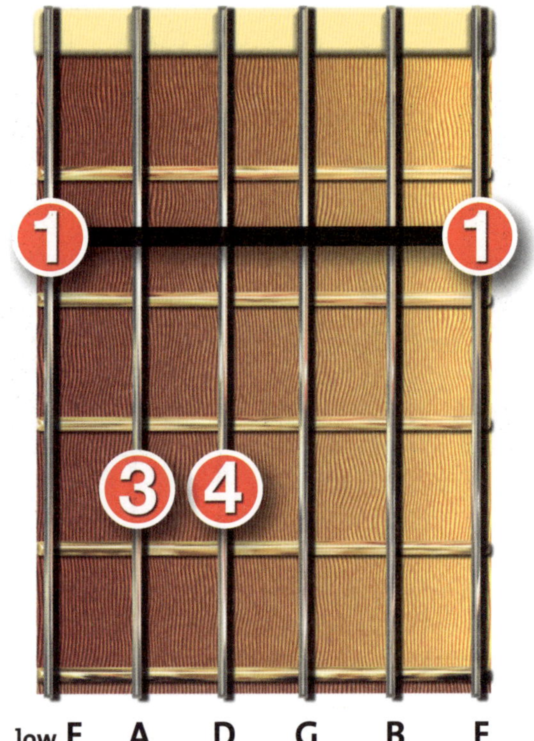

low E string A string D string G string B string E string

Guitar: first position.

1 index finger **2** middle finger **3** ring finger **4** little finger

Notes of the Chord

1st (F♯), ♭3rd (A), 5th (C♯)

F♯/G♭ G♯/A♭ A♯/B♭ C♯/D♭ D♯/E♭

1 4

2

F G A B C D E

Piano: right hand.

1 thumb **2** index finger **3** middle finger **4** ring finger **5** little finger

1
2
3
4
5
6
7
8
9
10
11
12

F♯sus4/G♭sus4

Suspended 4th

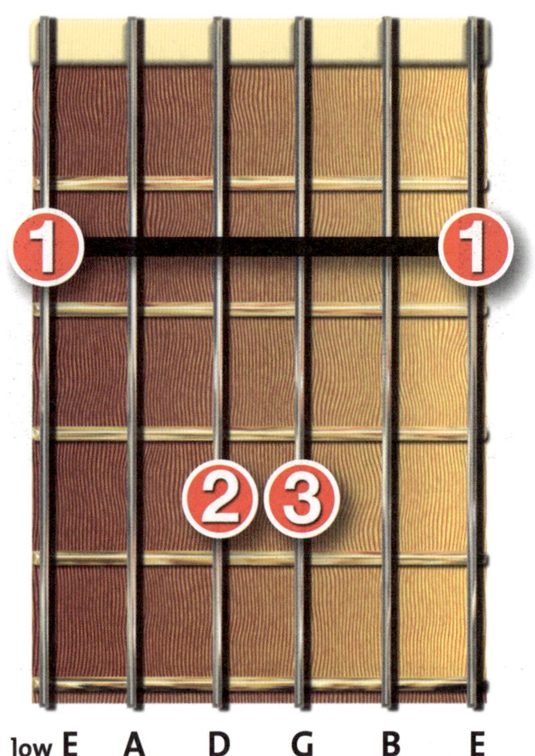

Guitar: first position.

1 index finger **2** middle finger **3** ring finger **4** little finger

Notes of the Chord

1st (F♯), 4th (B), 5th (C♯)

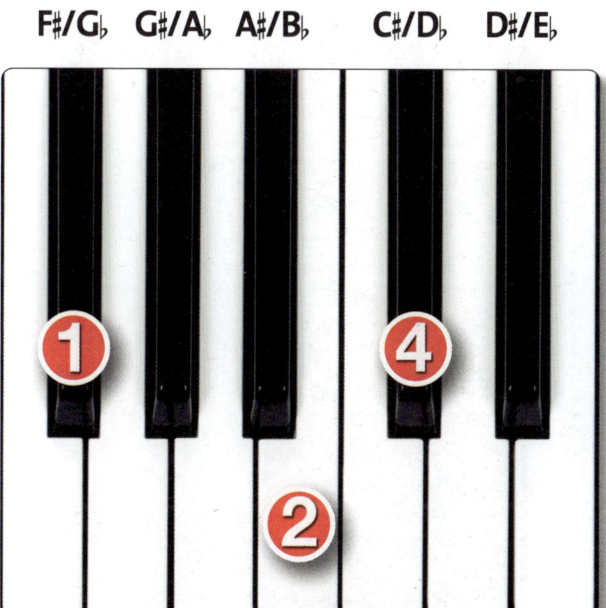

F G A B C D E

Piano: right hand.

1 thumb **2** index finger **3** middle finger **4** ring finger **5** little finger

F♯+/G♭+

Augmented

x x

2

low E string | A string | D string | G string | B string | E string

Guitar: first position.

1 index finger **2** middle finger **3** ring finger **4** little finger

Notes of the Chord

1st (F♯), 3rd (A♯), ♯5th (Cx)

F♯/G♭ G♯/A♭ A♯/B♭ C♯/D♭ D♯/E♭

1 2 4

F G A B C D E

Piano: right hand.

1 thumb **2** index finger **3** middle finger **4** ring finger **5** little finger

11

1
2
3
4
5
6
7
8
9
10
11
12

G

Major

Guitar: first position.

1 index finger **2** middle finger **3** ring finger **4** little finger

Notes of the Chord

1st (G), 3rd (B), 5th (D)

F♯/G♭ G♯/A♭ A♯/B♭ C♯/D♭ D♯/E♭

1 2 4

F G A B C D E

Piano: right hand.

1 thumb **2** index finger **3** middle finger **4** ring finger **5** little finger

1
2
3
4
5
6
7
8
9
10
11
12

Gm

Minor

3

low E string | A string | D string | G string | B string | E string

Guitar: first position.

1 index finger **2** middle finger **3** ring finger **4** little finger

Notes of the Chord

1st (G), ♭3rd (B♭), 5th (D)

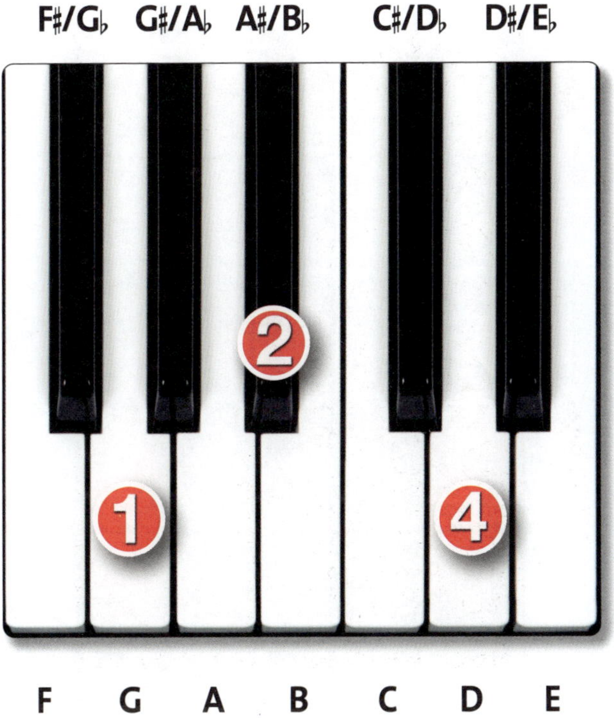

F♯/G♭ G♯/A♭ A♯/B♭ C♯/D♭ D♯/E♭

F G A B C D E

Piano: right hand.

1 thumb **2** index finger **3** middle finger **4** ring finger **5** little finger

1
2
3
4
5
6
7
8
9
10
11
12

Gsus4

Suspended 4th

X O O

1

3 4

low E string | A string | D string | G string | B string | E string

Guitar: first position.

1 index finger **2** middle finger **3** ring finger **4** little finger

Notes of the Chord

1st (G), 4th (C), 5th (D)

F♯/G♭ G♯/A♭ A♯/B♭ C♯/D♭ D♯/E♭

1 3 4

F G A B C D E

Piano: right hand.

1 thumb **2** index finger **3** middle finger **4** ring finger **5** little finger

G+

Augmented

X X

3

low E string | A string | D string | G string | B string | E string

Guitar: first position.

1 index finger **2** middle finger **3** ring finger **4** little finger

Notes of the Chord

1st (G), 3rd (B), ♯5th (D♯)

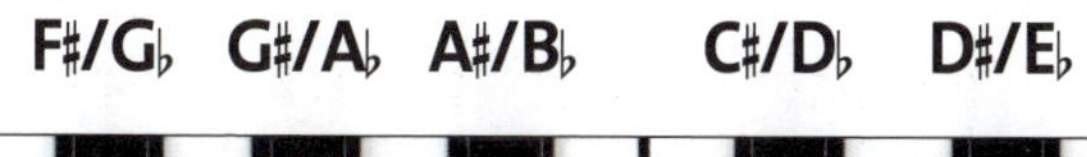

F G A B C D E

Piano: right hand.

1 thumb **2** index finger **3** middle finger **4** ring finger **5** little finger

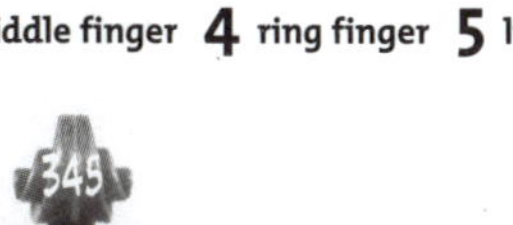

G♯/A♭

Major

low E string | A string | D string | G string | B string | E string

Guitar: first position.

1 index finger **2** middle finger **3** ring finger **4** little finger

Notes of the Chord

1st (A♭), 3rd (C), 5th (E♭)

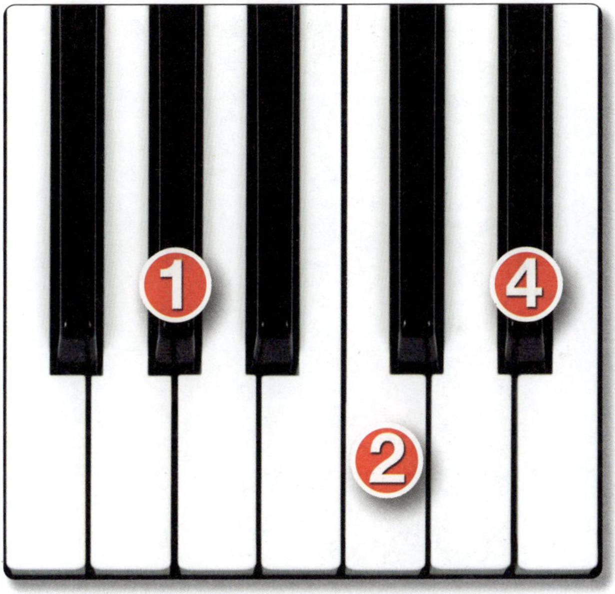
F♯/G♭
G♯/A♭
A♯/B♭
C♯/D♭
D♯/E♭
1
4
2
F
G
A
B
C
D
E

Piano: right hand.

1 thumb **2** index finger **3** middle finger **4** ring finger **5** little finger

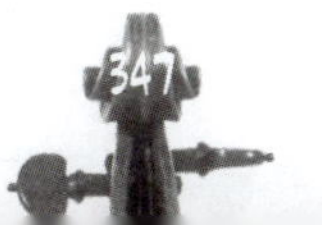

1
2
3
4
5
6
7
8
9
10
11
12

G♯m/A♭m

Minor

low E string | A string | D string | G string | B string | E string

Guitar: first position.

1 index finger **2** middle finger **3** ring finger **4** little finger

Notes of the Chord

1st (A♭), ♭3rd (C♭), 5th (E♭)

1
2
3
4
5
6
7
8
9
10
11
12

Piano: right hand.

1 thumb **2** index finger **3** middle finger **4** ring finger **5** little finger

1
2
3
4
5
6
7
8
9
10
11
12

G♯sus4/A♭sus4

Suspended 4th

low E string A string D string G string B string E string

Guitar: first position.

1 index finger **2** middle finger **3** ring finger **4** little finger

Notes of the Chord

1st (A♭), 4th (D♭), 5th (E♭)

Piano: right hand.

1 thumb **2** index finger **3** middle finger **4** ring finger **5** little finger

G♯+/A♭+

Augmented

low E string | A string | D string | G string | B string | E string

Guitar: first position.

1 index finger **2** middle finger **3** ring finger **4** little finger

11

Notes of the Chord

1st (A♭), 3rd (C), ♯5th (E)

F♯/G♭ G♯/A♭ A♯/B♭ C♯/D♭ D♯/E♭

1 2 4

F G A B C D E

Piano: right hand.

1 thumb **2** index finger **3** middle finger **4** ring finger **5** little finger

A

Major

X O O

low E string | A string | D string | G string | B string | E string

Guitar: first position.

1 index finger **2** middle finger **3** ring finger **4** little finger

Notes of the Chord

1st (A), 3rd (C♯), 5th (E)

F♯/G♭ G♯/A♭ A♯/B♭ C♯/D♭ D♯/E♭

2

1 4

F G A B C D E

Piano: right hand.

1 thumb **2** index finger **3** middle finger **4** ring finger **5** little finger

Am

Minor

low E	A	D	G	B	E
string	string	string	string	string	string

Guitar: first position.

1 index finger **2** middle finger **3** ring finger **4** little finger

Notes of the Chord

1st (A), ♭3rd (C), 5th (E)

F♯/G♭ G♯/A♭ A♯/B♭ C♯/D♭ D♯/E♭

1 2 4

F G A B C D E

Piano: right hand.

1 thumb **2** index finger **3** middle finger **4** ring finger **5** little finger

Asus4

Suspended 4th

Guitar: first position.

1 index finger **2** middle finger **3** ring finger **4** little finger

Notes of the Chord

1st (A), 4th (D), 5th (E)

F♯/G♭ G♯/A♭ A♯/B♭ C♯/D♭ D♯/E♭

1 2 3

F G A B C D E

Piano: right hand.

1 thumb **2** index finger **3** middle finger **4** ring finger **5** little finger

1
2
3
4
5
6
7
8
9
10
11
12

A+

Augmented

low E string | A string | D string | G string | B string | E string

Guitar: first position.

1 index finger **2** middle finger **3** ring finger **4** little finger

Notes of the Chord

1st (A), 3rd (C♯), ♯5th (E♯)

A♯/B♭ C♯/D♭ D♯/E♭ F♯/G♭

A B C D E F G

Piano: right hand.

1 thumb **2** index finger **3** middle finger **4** ring finger **5** little finger

1 2 3 4 5 6 7 8 9 10 11 12

A♯/B♭

Major

low E string | A string | D string | G string | B string | E string

Guitar: first position.

1 index finger **2** middle finger **3** ring finger **4** little finger

Notes of the Chord

1st (B♭), 3rd (D), 5th (F)

A♯/B♭ C♯/D♭ D♯/E♭ F♯/G♭

1 2 4

A B C D E F G

Piano: right hand.

1 thumb **2** index finger **3** middle finger **4** ring finger **5** little finger

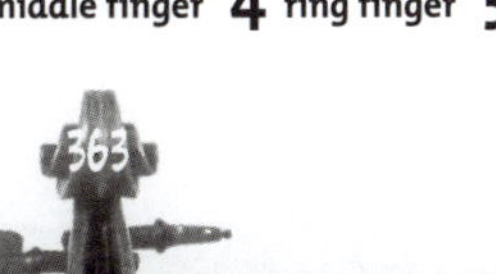

A♯m/B♭m

Minor

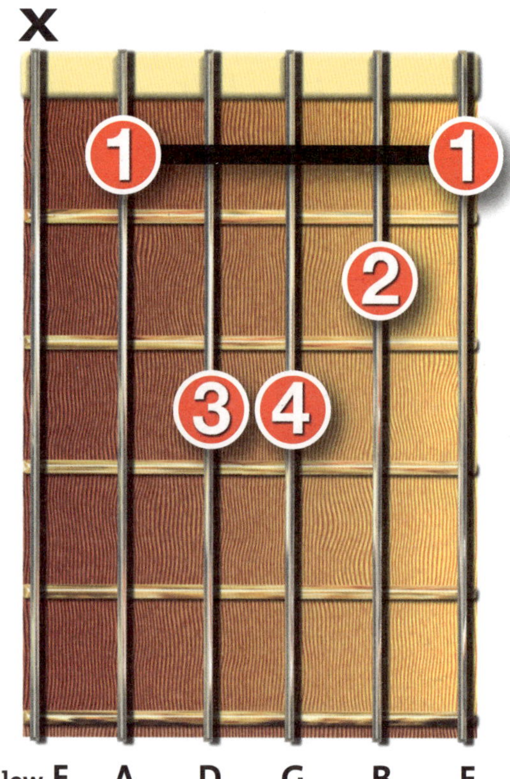

Guitar: first position.

1 index finger **2** middle finger **3** ring finger **4** little finger

Notes of the Chord

1st (B♭), ♭3rd (D♭), 5th (F)

A♯/B♭ C♯/D♭ D♯/E♭ F♯/G♭

1 2 4

A B C D E F G

Piano: right hand.

1 thumb **2** index finger **3** middle finger **4** ring finger **5** little finger

A♯sus4/B♭sus4

Suspended 4th

low E string | A string | D string | G string | B string | E string

Guitar: first position.

1 index finger **2** middle finger **3** ring finger **4** little finger

Notes of the Chord

1st (B♭), 4th (E♭), 5th (F)

A♯/B♭ C♯/D♭ D♯/E♭ F♯/G♭

1 3 4

A B C D E F G

Piano: right hand.

1 thumb **2** index finger **3** middle finger **4** ring finger **5** little finger

A♯+/B♭+

Augmented

3

low E string | A string | D string | G string | B string | E string

Guitar: first position.

1 index finger **2** middle finger **3** ring finger **4** little finger

Notes of the Chord

1st (B♭), 3rd (D), ♯5th (F♯)

A♯/B♭ C♯/D♭ D♯/E♭ F♯/G♭

1 4 2

A B C D E F G

Piano: right hand.

1 thumb **2** index finger **3** middle finger **4** ring finger **5** little finger

B

Major

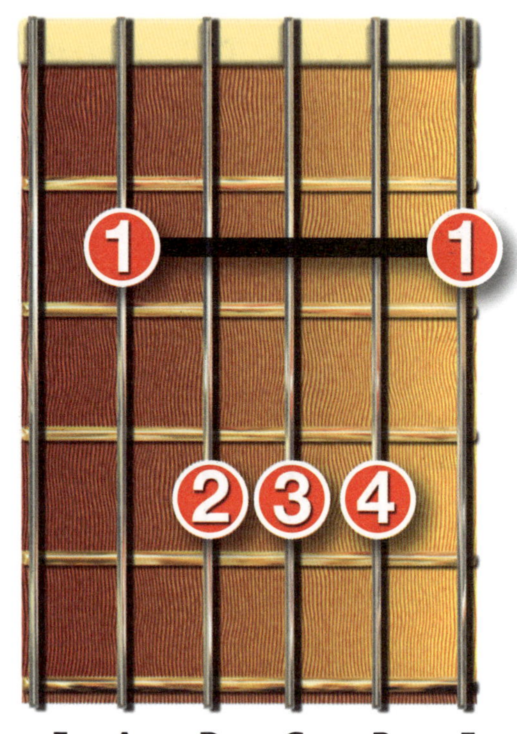

low **E** string | **A** string | **D** string | **G** string | **B** string | **E** string

Guitar: first position.

1 index finger **2** middle finger **3** ring finger **4** little finger

Notes of the Chord

1st (B), 3rd (D♯), 5th (F♯)

A♯/B♭ C♯/D♭ D♯/E♭ F♯/G♭

3 4

1

A B C D E F G

Piano: right hand.

1 thumb **2** index finger **3** middle finger **4** ring finger **5** little finger

Bm

Minor

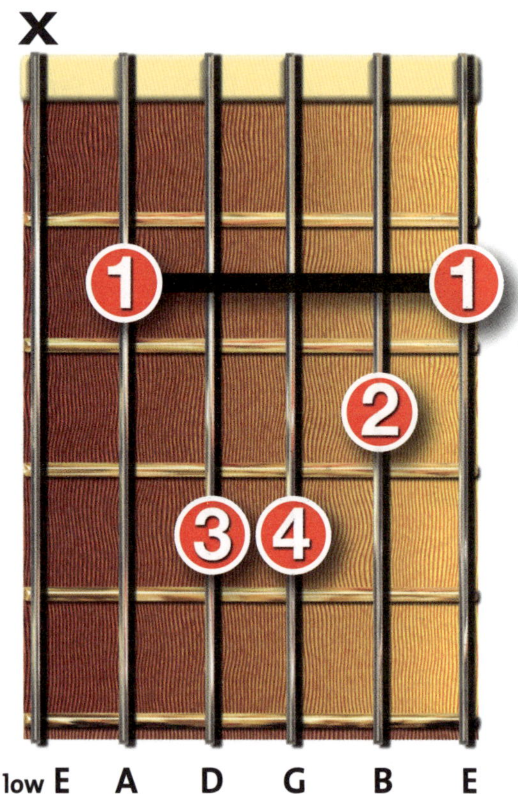

low E string | A string | D string | G string | B string | E string

Guitar: first position.

1 index finger **2** middle finger **3** ring finger **4** little finger

Notes of the Chord

1st (B), ♭3rd (D), 5th (F♯)

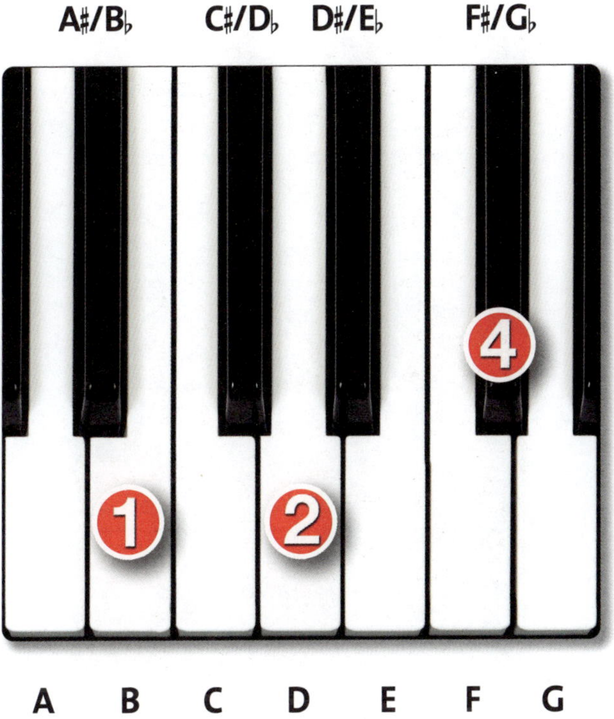

A♯/B♭ C♯/D♭ D♯/E♭ F♯/G♭

A B C D E F G

Piano: right hand.

1 thumb **2** index finger **3** middle finger **4** ring finger **5** little finger

Bsus4

Suspended 4th

X

2

low **E** string | **A** string | **D** string | **G** string | **B** string | **E** string

Guitar: first position.

1 index finger **2** middle finger **3** ring finger **4** little finger

Notes of the Chord

1st (B), 4th (E), 5th (F♯)

A♯/B♭ C♯/D♭ D♯/E♭ F♯/G♭

1 3 4

A B C D E F G

Piano: right hand.

1 thumb **2** index finger **3** middle finger **4** ring finger **5** little finger

B+

Augmented

4

low E string | A string | D string | G string | B string | E string

Guitar: first position.

1 index finger **2** middle finger **3** ring finger **4** little finger

Notes of the Chord

1st (B), 3rd (D), ♯5th (Fx)

A♯/B♭ C♯/D♭ D♯/E♭ F♯/G♭

1 2 4

A B C D E F G

Piano: right hand.

1 thumb **2** index finger **3** middle finger **4** ring finger **5** little finger

1 2 3 4 5 6 7 8 9 10 11 12

12

Symbols & Marks

Step 12

A musical piece is often full of symbols, all of which provide clues about how the music should be played: how loud, what speed and when to repeat.

Classical music uses a great many Italian terms because in the early 1600s Italy was the cultural centre of European music. Church choral music moved to broader orchestral forms, the major and minor scales were standardized and tonal music gained great influence, resulting in the western classical style. The twentieth century brought an explosion of new styles of music (blues, jazz, rock) and with them the greater use of English terms.

Tempo

These marks are written above the music and show how quickly to play the music.

lento or ***adagio***	slowly
andante	at walking speed
moderato	at a moderate speed
allegretto	fairly fast
allegro	fast
presto	very fast
ritardando (***rit.***)	slowing down
accelerando (***accel.***)	getting faster
a tempo	at original speed
piu mosso	faster
meno mosso	slower
ad lib./ad libitum	freely

Dynamics

These marks are written underneath the notes and show how loudly to play the music.

pp	***pianissimo***	very quiet
p	***piano***	quiet
mp	***mezzopiano***	fairly quiet
mf	***mezzoforte***	fairly loud
f	***forte***	loud
ff	***fortissimo***	very loud
<	***crescendo*** (***cresc***.)	growing louder
>	***diminuendo*** (***dim***.)	growing quieter

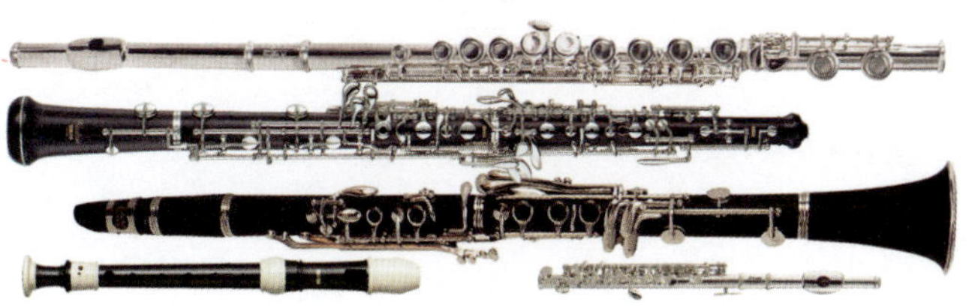

Articulation

These marks are written above or underneath the notes and show how to play the notes.

Mark	Term	Meaning
.	***staccato***	short
>	***accento***	accented
Λ	***marcato***	louder accent
—	***tenuto***	slightly stressed
⁀	***legato***	slur, smooth
sfz	***sforzando***	forced, heavy accent
fp	***fortepiano***	loud attack then quiet
𝄐	***fermata***	hold, pause
8va	***all‘ ottava***	One octave higher than written
8vb	***ottava bassa***	One octave lower than written
tr~~~~~~~~		trill

Other Symbols

D.C. al Fine	Return to the beginning and play to ***Fine*** (end).
D.S. al Fine	Return to 𝄋 and play to ***Fine.***
D.C. al Coda	Return to the beginning, play to 𝄌 and skip to Coda.
D.S. al Coda	Return to 𝄋 , play to 𝄌 and skip to Coda.
:‖	Return to the beginning or nearest repeat sign. ‖:

Stems and Beams

Notes below the third line are written with their stems up. For beamed notes, the note furthest from the third line determines the stem direction.

Further Reading and other useful internet resources for this book are available on **www.flametreemusic.com**

The Beginner's Guide to Reading Music is another in our best-selling series of easy-to-use music books designed for players of all abilities and ages. Created for musicians by musicians, these books offer a quick and practical resource for those playing on their own or with a band. They work equally well for the rock and indie musician as they do for the jazz, folk, country, blues or classical enthusiast.

FlameTreeMusic.com

Flame Tree Music offers useful, practical information on chords, scales, riffs, rhymes and instruments through a growing combination of traditional print books and ebooks.

Books in the series:

Advanced Guitar Chords; Guitar Chords; Piano & Keyboard Chords; Chords for Kids; Play Flamenco; How to Play Guitar; How to Play Bass Guitar; How to Play Piano; How to Play Classic Riffs; Songwriter's Rhyming Dictionary; How to Become a Star; How to Read Music; How to Write Great Songs; How to Play Rock Rhythm, Riffs & Lead; How to Play Hard, Metal & Nu Rock; How to Make Music on the Web; My First Recorder Music; Piano Sheet Music; Brass & Wind Sheet Music; Scales & Modes.

For further information on these titles please visit our trading website: www.flametreepublishing.com